Radical Empathy in Leadership

EQUITY-FOCUSED TESTIMONIALS, TRIALS, & TOOLS FOR SCHOOL LEADERS

Dr. Ian Roberts

Cover and interior book design:
Ashley Gaffney Design (AGD Studio)

Radical Empathy in Leadership: Equity-Focused Testimonials, Trails, and Tools for School Leaders by Dr. Ian A. Roberts 1st ed.

ISBN-13: 9798718962765

Photography courtesy of UnSplash: Charles Deluvio (p. 15), Steven Lelham (p. 25), Alexis Chloe (p. 33), Markus Spiske (p. 40, 169), Tim Marshall (p. 53), Kiana Bosman (p. 63), Nikita Kachanovsky (p. 76), Annie Spratt (p. 96), Thought Catalog (p. 122), Isaac Smith (p. 134), LaTerrian McIntosh (p. 145), Joshua Hoehne (p. 159), Olena Sergienko (p. 184), Reuben Juarez (p. 190), Tyler Nix (p. 198)

Radical Empathy in Leadership

EQUITY-FOCUSED TESTIMONIALS, TRIALS, & TOOLS FOR SCHOOL LEADERS

Dr. Ian Roberts

This work is dedicated to the woman who epitomizes what it means to be a radically empathetic human being, and who is my first teacher—my mother Verna Elvira Roberts.

Table of Contents

Foreward

I was skeptical when Dr. Ian Roberts first mentioned the radical empathy concept to me in a random meeting in an airport in Charlotte, NC. Afterall, just a few years prior, I had been aptly named "The Nic-A-Nator" and I was proud of it. It was a play on words between my actual name and the fictional character played by Arnold Schwarzenegger - The Terminator. In essence, it is a gross understatement to say that I have not always led with empathy. Nonetheless, Dr. Roberts made a compelling case for radical empathy by sharing a few examples of how this approach was the pathway to the success of his teams. Although I was skeptical, I am not known to be resistant to evidence-based and proven methods. Therefore, I took him up on his offer to learn more concerning what the fuss was all about.

I sat in an audience watching as hundreds of educators pondered in reflection. They had been asked by Dr. Ian Roberts to "think of a time when someone gave [them] an opportunity that perhaps [they] did not deserve." For me there was too much discomfort in the silence but when volunteers began to vulnerably share their personal histories, my life began to transform. Often emotional, many participants shared stories riddled with unconscionable behavior and then went on to describe how the grace of another person set them on a different path. They weren't sharing how getting fired changed them. They weren't offering up examples of how being canceled inspired them to do or be different. Instead, it was "far reaching" or "extreme" empathy from others that made the difference in their lives.

I find empathy or understanding to be effortless to demonstrate when I feel like someone deserves my understanding or my grace. But what happens when I believe a person, or a group doesn't deserve anything from me let alone *radical empathy*? It can be a challenging position to find yourself in when you value uplifting the human spirit. People have many reasons for sometimes missing the mark and it is in those moments when they need grace the most. I'm embarrassed to admit that in the past I rarely chose radical empathy. In fact, I often found it much easier to make decisions that leaned more on deservedness rather than choosing a more gracious approach. Nonetheless, I've come a long way since I met Dr. Roberts in

2014. However, at that time my already entrenched leadership journey was still fraught with occasion after occasion of me questioning where the line was when people consistently did things to disappoint me. But at every turn since then I could hear Dr. Roberts challenging me to not only seek to understand but to do so to the extreme - *radically*.

I have gotten more feedback than I care to share about my need to be more emotionally intelligent. I have spent years reading about the topic and trying to implement the methods. In fact I have read hundreds of leadership books and research articles on the subject. In all, I still struggled to hold people to a high standard and also show up in ways that demonstrated that I authentically cared about them. However, since practicing the radical empathy strategies I have seen a difference in myself but more importantly, I have positively impacted the lives of others in ways that I could not have before.

Unlike him I have never been a teacher in K-12 education. Yet, I fully appreciate those of you who decide to serve our nation's most vulnerable - our children. You are inherently better positioned for this work than I ever was or ever could be. So here is my charge to you, take heed to the examples in these writings and truly dissect the stories. First, because in over a decade, there hasn't been one time where being relentless about my need to understand another person has gotten me into trouble. Secondly, because the leaders I interact with every day are depending on you to save us all. They regularly share that their "kids are learning to be better in school." They believe that you are demonstrating for our young people exactly how to be better, more empathetic humans in the sea of people-failures and disappointments. Lastly, I invite you to embrace radical empathy because if a hard nosed leader like myself can pivot towards a more radically empathetic stance, anyone can - especially you!

Dr. Nicole D. Price

Owner and CEO of the leadership development company,
Lively Paradox

Preface

At 22 years old, I successfully graduated from Officer Candidate School which was purported to be the most rigorous military training program in the western hemisphere. After receiving my commission from the president, I led the Quick Reaction Group (QRG) or "Black Clothes." One of the other less affectionate names used to refer to the QRG was "The Death Squad." In this role, I served on the security detail for Queen Elizabeth II during her first visit to the English-speaking Caribbean in fifty years. My training required me to defend people like the Queen by any means necessary - including stopping or killing any person or group threatening that security. Protecting the interest of the government was my main concern. During this time, empathy was not at the forefront of my leadership.

Neuroscientists tell us that 98% of people can be empathetic. I instinctively knew that I was a part of that 98% while leading the QRG. This unit patrolled and targeted the continent's most dangerous criminals. The team had many instances when the sergeant on the night shift would wake me during the wee hours of the morning to share their critical incident report. In this report, I would receive a detailed account of the melee or occurrences from the patrols. They would regularly share other aspects of the shift as well. On many occasions, the report included explanatory notes about a fatality involving a wanted criminal at the hands of unit personnel. After receiving the report from the sergeant in charge of the shift, my first reaction was to personally examine the entry and exit wounds of the deceased. My purpose was to check for consistency with the accompanying narrative and action. There were too many instances when there were inconsistencies. The story of the reporting officer and fatal wounds of the deceased just didn't match. This caused me to make several disciplinary decisions and, in many instances, remove officers from our team. Although the victims were men and women with lengthy criminal histories, I believed that they deserved due process, and more importantly, to be treated as human beings. These actions were indications that focusing on empathy was possible for me although I didn't overtly express the idea at the time. My history of being a trained assassin is important because people believe that I have always had a "soft" heart towards the needs of others. I have not. Furthermore, in pursuit of racial equity, school leaders are not faced with "Death Squad" situations however, the challenges are no less important and require radical empathy.

Everyone in the United States is a participant in, competitor against, or audience member in the fight for racial equity. One of the most prevalent contributing factors of pervasive racial inequities in the United States is the unwillingness to recognize the humanity of others. Individuals who subscribe to white supremacist culture have made it pellucidly clear through daily actions and institutionalized structures that they will not recognize persons of color as their equal intellectually, physically, or politically. There is a plethora of research that disputes this thinking. Despite the evidence that displays the incredible accomplishments of persons of color, there is an unwillingness to acknowledge the need for race equity. The pervasiveness of these challenges speaks to a lack of empathy at the most basic levels.

Racial inequity in all institutions is the most pressing civil rights issue of our time. In schools, we have an issue to resolve that actively involves all of us. You do not get to opt out. The role you assume in the fight for racial equity is built on the choices that you make, and in many instances, the role you are assigned. There must be an acknowledgement that each of us in this arena has arrived at this point in our lives via vastly different and unique paths. I share my experiences as a commissioned military officer, Olympic athlete, special education teacher, school, and district leader with the intention that it will provide you with a front row seat into my journey of becoming a radically empathetic practitioner in the fight for racial equity in schools. I hope to inspire you to come along with me and if you have surpassed me, bring others along.

Introduction

School leaders make an average of 500 decisions that affect thousands of people daily. These decisions are coupled with developing partnerships and a host of other undertakings that include:

- interactions with internal and external stakeholders

- conducting leadership observations

- Individualized Education Plans (IEP) meetings

- disciplinary referrals

- vertical teaming meetings

- scheduling decisions

- attendance at athletic activities

- data meetings

- parent meetings

Given the magnitude of these daily responsibilities, our decisions are grounded in the technical aspects of our work to operationalize the results. These technical aspects are often narrowly focused on the strategic planning outcomes. Frequently, those same technical aspects, even while being detailed in the strategic plans, are misaligned to the daily actions of the professionals asked to implement them. This myopic focus on technical work has been the practice of school and district leaders for decades, yet the plight of growing inequities in the education systems in the U.S. remains present. Although not a panacea, one approach to resolving this issue is the need to anchor our work in an empathy-based approach. To be clear, I do not mean to simply pivot towards empathy. I am advocating for radical empathy in leadership to transform our daily practices. Making this pivot is critical to dismantling the racial inequalities that have persistently plagued us.

I will not attempt to make the shift to become radically empathetic seem like an easy undertaking. It is not. It is not easy because the work environment in K-12 education often discourages leading and teaching from the heart. Too often the people who have committed to serve students and families face the high stakes accountability nature of the U.S. K-12 education system. Our system is one that over indexes on decision making that is anchored and driven by data. This overt focus on data-driven decisions (rather than people-centric decisions) further perpetuates the racialized outcomes that oppress marginalized groups. It forces its participants to become pre-occupied with protecting their status and privilege, their own beliefs, professional trajectory, and essentially, self-preservation at all cost. Working in a culture that elevates meritocracy and bureaucratic pressure for participants, who has time to exercise empathy and compassion?

Compassion is the verb-alignment of empathy. As described in *Mindful of Race*, Ruth King describes compassion as "literally meaning to suffer with others, to feel what they feel." King shares that the Hebrew word for compassion is derived from the word "womb." Thus, compassion for someone is tantamount to the feeling that a mother would have for her child. As educators, we are the teachers and parents outside the home. We make personal connections and build trusting, authentic relationships with students when we are compassionate towards them. These displays will in turn activate the empathy gene in our students who are recipients of our compassion. It is often said that children do not care what you know until they really know that you care. Our children may not do what the adults around them say, but they are certainly inclined to repeat all the actions of the adults. Radical empathy is a verb that considers and requires authentic action. Children, especially during their formative years are likely to grow into empathetic adolescents and eventually, radically empathetic adults. Unfortunately, they are not capable of activating their own empathy muscles, we have to help them to do so.

I am often described in many education circles as a relentless qualitative researcher who shares my practical experiences in stories and vignettes. I am confident that the appetite educators have for quantitative data and statistical validity can be found in the stories in this book. I have taken great care to share quantitative data references that will likely resonate with theoreticians. But I have also combined specific, real-life case studies that will satisfy the pragmatists and day-to-day practitioners serving in leadership roles. I will consistently use stories to connect empathy, in the radical sense, to racial, cultural, and academic equity progress in education. This catalog of "quick-reads" and reflective writings is designed to refresh and stretch the empathetic and equity-focused leadership muscles and mental models you might have.

I am not sharing from an academic or theoretician lens. I have been blessed to offer life-changing pedagogical direction and leadership in many spaces. It has truly been a privilege and blessing to have served in roles ranging from a special education teacher to a district administrator in almost every region in the United States, espousing bold and radical leadership in each situation. My time of teaching and leading in eleven school districts, many of them serving marginalized students, resulted in radically changing the focus of districts. This change in focus positively changed the lives of thousands of students and the amazing adults who served them. Teachers, administrators, and paraprofessionals can use the techniques I share to enhance empathy in their professional and personal lives.

I passionately believe in the trickle down effect. Consequently, I am convinced that as the adults in our school building get better the children will experience dramatically different and much improved outcomes. I am passionate about changing the lives of teachers and students as we look to the next phase of radical change in the K-12 educational arena in this country.

Caution

The stories captured in the upcoming writings will unapologetically address the prevalence and impact of racialized outcomes and inequities in K-12 education. I will make certain assertions that will undoubtedly result in emotions like anger, passion, sympathy, sadness, and resentment. My plan is to push you so that you have an unapologetic willingness to discuss privilege, racism, bigotry, and bias. My hope is that your social activism will include radical empathy in leadership.

Chapter 1.

The Road to the Olympics

If there was ever an oxymoron that thoughtfully conflates the necessity for activism and the work of leading from the heart, it is the term *radical empathy in leadership*. Many people have asked about my motivation for elevating this term, its connection to race equity, and challenged me to unpack this idea and my accompanying philosophy. In response, I always preface the ensuing debate with a simple phrase —"You have to understand my journey in order to appreciate my passion." For those of us who are charged with leading schools, it is critical that we do so only after attempting to understand the stories of teachers and students and understand their purposes for being or their WHY. My WHY has a slightly different beginning from many of my counterparts in U.S. educational leadership.

I am the grandson of a rice-paddy and coconut farmer and the son of a phenomenal woman and seamstress from Guyana, South America. My country of origin is geographically located on the coast of South America and is home to the only English-speaking people on the continent. Guyanese people are politically and culturally affiliated with the Caribbean because of the Treaty of Chaguaramas signed on July 4, 1973. The treaty between Guyana, Barbados, Jamaica, and Trinidad & Tobago created the union of CARICOM. The Caribbean Community and

Common Market (CARICOM) is a group of twenty developing countries in the Caribbean that have come together to form an economic and political community that works together to shape policies for the region and encourages economic growth and trade.

The culture often elevated in Guyana was one where my family members and neighbors exhibited unselfishness and empathy in every way possible. My mother would often deprive herself to provide for someone else; relative or stranger. I believe that my radical empathetic orientation had its genesis during those years. A significant portion of youth was spent in Guyana. Like many people, my formative years are still influencing my current perspective.

Simon Sinek states in his book *Start with WHY* that although many of us find our WHY during our formative years, it does not typically manifest itself until several years later. As a result of 25 years of various professional experiences prior to education, I am finally in a place where I have a laser focus on my WHY. It is a focus that is anchored in a strategic approach to intersect radical empathy, racial equity, and mission-focused leadership, and it began in the Caribbean.

Even with such great examples from my formative years, I am the first to confess that I still have not always been an empathetic leader. While I was empathetic to strangers, I did not always extend the same courtesy to my team of educators or even to students. I have spent too much time being culturally destructive and it took lots of heart wrenching experiences, sometimes at the expense of children, for me to move closer to radical empathy. For this reason, I will often call out the fact that all of us are at varying places on a vast continuum from cultural destruction to being effective, empathetic, and culturally responsive teachers and leaders. Radical empathy is critical to helping us move along the continuum in a positive direction.

In your current role, it is incredibly beneficial to you and those you serve if you can reflect on that moment in your history when your journey started. It will also help to identify where you are on the continuum of empathy and culturally responsiveness. In his bestselling book, *Discovering Your Why*, Simon Sinek shares that our WHY is discovered as early as our 15th birthday and it never changes. It is highly likely that you will see a strong connection to your discovery on this continuum to your life's purpose or the finding of your WHY - the reason for your passion, commitment, and convictions about a particular pursuit, or the lack thereof.

Although Sinek's assertion about identifying your WHY by age 15 years old may generally hold true, my discovery of purpose or my WHY came much later. My journey as a radically empathetic leader was discovered in my 20s although it did not manifest itself until a decade later during my tenure as a high school principal in Washington, DC. In 2000, I competed as a track and field athlete in the Olympic Games in Sydney, Australia. The dreams and plans we have for our lives are often far from accurate. My athletic path and my educational leadership journey provide an example of how far-off track we can be with our disjointed or seemingly disconnected projections. Often this disconnect can be attributed to the lack of maturity and cognitive establishment that surrounds our life.

My mother, during her hundreds of moments of enlightening and instructive guidance through lessons, quotes, and fables often reminded me that "if you want to make God laugh, share your plans." Her point was that although we may make plans based on our desires, personal and professional circles, and academic qualifications, who we become and what passion we pursue has already been predetermined. Yes, she believes, and now so do I, that there is divine guidance, intervention, and interruption that dictates what we will spend most of our waking moments doing in the future. I know for certain that my mother's wisdom about divine guidance was being validated by the time I reached my mid-30s.

My mother, deceased father, and my brothers are amongst some of the most brilliant humans I have known, yet none of them have ever set foot on a college or university campus. However, I am honored to stand on their shoulders. But seven years prior to my participation in the Olympic Games, no one could have convinced me that I would become an elite athlete - acknowledged and celebrated for being in the top 2% of athletes on the world stage. As a first-generation college student, I recognized that my desire for a post-secondary education was likely to be impeded by my family's inability to afford college for me and my siblings. An athletic ability, affinity for reading, sapiosexual inclination, and proclivity for intellectual stimulation served as catalysts for my entry into college, thereby breaking our family's experience with unattainable college education.

I was certainly an "at-promise" (opposed to at-risk) youth

while living in Crown-Heights Brooklyn. However, my summer track and field club coach encouraged me to explore how my athletic talent could gain me a free college education. At the end of the summer track and field season, we embarked on an aggressive college recruitment and application tour. Disappointingly, we were promptly rejected by the first four colleges I was interested in within a 24-hour period. At the end of that day though, my luck would change, or as my mother would say, divine intervention granted me grace.

On our way back to New York, we visited the fifth college - Coppin State. In my mind that was likely my last opportunity to enroll in college on a scholarship. Miraculously, the Coppin State coach saw the promise in me and offered a full athletic and academic scholarship. That day in Baltimore, Maryland will forever stand out in my mind. Here I was at my wits-end and someone took a chance on me. He was understanding. He was radically empathetic when he didn't have to be and with no knowledge of whether or not his decision would pay off.

The final experience was inspiring because when I arrived in Baltimore, I was disheartened by all of the previous rejection from college coaches. What stood out the most was that there was not an ounce of empathy in the conversations with any of the other coaches. The previous four coaches cared nothing about me or my potential as they shared their own sentiments:

"You are not running fast enough." "You can walk on to the team and maybe we will consider giving you books next year." "You are not good enough." "We have girls on our track team who run faster than you."

However, one inspiring action I took from those rejections was a determination to prove them wrong with my ability every chance I got after that experience. It may have been an immature response, but I was determined to make them regret their choices and that I did. I never lost an 800-meter race to any student-athlete from any of those four schools throughout my collegiate track career.

The coach at Coppin State gave me a chance but not without an ask. He requested that I commit to working hard. I promised him and the team that I would train harder than anyone they knew and give 100% every day. A man's word is his bond. Yes, as cliché as it sounds, I kept my promise to my coach and teammates simply because I did not want to return to Brooklyn as a failure. I made this promise because I knew this was once in a once in a life-time opportunity and potentially a life-changing experience for me and my family, too. I spent the next four years training and working out relentlessly while completing rigorous coursework.

One of the lessons that I learned and have come to appreciate is that college persistence for many students who share my story is contingent on more than academic ability. It requires a preparation that builds their resilience muscles and commitment to succeed. For many first-generation college students, persistence can often be thwarted by peers and family members encouraging you to "leave college for a bit" and explore other options such as finding a job when things get "hard," and they will get "hard." In many instances, there are no models or examples for you to seek out for guidance. I realized and decided that persistence is critical to change one's life circumstance. Regardless of your lived experience, be it a first-generation college student or someone for whom college attendance and graduation is the tradition in your family, life's curve balls, challenges, and change are inevitable. We must remember that the desire to persist is innate in each of us. One key to activate our persistence muscles and to increase self-awareness is to use an approach that my friend and colleague Dr. Nicole Price in the bestselling book, "The Power of Seven Second Chances" calls ARDAC (Awareness, Reflection, Decision, Action, Check).

This approach inspires you to tap into an **Awareness** of your own life circumstance, **Reflect** on what your previous and current realities are, **Decide** to do something about (consider several options), take very specific **Action** to change your reality to persists in the face of the challenge or change, and continuously **Check** at intervals to see how your persistence strategy is working. My use of **ARDAC**, coupled with my commitment to be the first in my family to graduate from college resulted in me becoming a relatively successful collegiate athlete, and eventually qualifying for the 2000 Olympic Games.

Chapter 2.

How I Became an Educator

I arrived in Sydney, Australia in the summer of 2000 ready to compete at the highest level. More importantly, I was confident that I would become an Olympic finalist and possibly win an Olympic medal. This confidence was based on the trend data that was unearthed from my performance statistics during the two years prior to the games:

1. I was ranked as the 8th fastest 800 meter runner in the world during one season.

2. I had competed in two World Championships in Maebashi, Japan and Seville, Spain.

3. I was a Pan American Games finalist.

4. I had won the gold medal at the Central American Championships in Bridgetown, Barbados.

Given the season's success, I was poised to compete at my best and run well. Then life happened. In front of an audience of thousands of people in the stadium and millions around the world watching on television, I failed. But it was there that I truly discovered my WHY.

At the 110-meter mark in the 800 meter race, there was some pushing and tripping amongst athletes as a result of R. Botha, the world champion athlete from South-Africa, cutting into the first lane prematurely. After an inadvertent push from behind, one leg collided with the other, my hamstring immediately knotted, and I felt as if I was physically incapable of moving. In fact, I do not remember where I got the strength to jog the remaining 700 meters to finish the race, but I was committed to doing so. Regardless of my mental strength, years of training and preparation for any eventuality, my Olympic dreams were over. At the time, I experienced the event as more than a failure *I* felt like a failure.

Prior to my arrival in Sydney, I had spent the previous two years finishing graduate school in Queens, New York. The academic program was rigorous but still I trained three times a day, six days a week. My training sessions started at 6AM with weights, conditioning, and plyometrics. The second session was at 3PM with track and field repetitions or distance conditioning. I ended my day with a midnight session that consisted of more technical repetitions, mental visualizations, and race assimilations. My training routine and commitment to becoming the best in the world started to pay dividends.

As one can imagine, I approached the Olympic Games healthy and brimming with confidence. I had trained for this moment. This race was slated to be the fastest preliminary 800m race because the lineup included the current world record holder, precious world champion, and the silver medalist from the 1996 Olympic Games. I was excited, thrilled, and wound up with anticipation. I honestly believed that I would make the finals. Then the memorable and life changing incident happened.

One take away from being tripped in the race is that no amount of preparation can get you ready for life's most unpredictable events. Once I completed the race, jogging to the sympathy applause of the spectators, I walked off the track. There, I was immediately approached by two credentialed officials who informed me that I was randomly selected for drug testing. My coach and I were then escorted to the space behind the competition track where we spent the next twenty minutes going through the process of the random drug test. Incidentally, the rules of the International Olympic Committee (IOC) state that an athlete whose progress was impeded through no fault of their own could file an appeal if done so within minutes. The other athlete in the race who was impeded, my peer from the Jamaican team, filed an appeal within the appropriate time and was reinstated to the next round. Moments later, after successfully passing the drug screen, I was informed that I missed the appeal window.

In that moment I realized that all hope for a redo was over. I walked out of the arena embarrassed. Seated in the back of a shuttle bus with my head covered in my hooded jacket, I made my way back to the Olympic village. Once there, I stayed in my room for three days, crying and envisioning every possible what-if scenario. I only left my room during the wee hours of the morning to get snacks from the vending machines. I wanted to avoid any conversations with anyone about what happened. My Olympic spirit was deflated, I booked an early flight back to the States, and skipped the closing ceremony.

Once home, I spent the next several weeks locked away in my apartment with my roommate and friend Dr. Damion Kenwood. He tried hard but none of his words of encouragement were not enough to get me moving. In my despair, I heard an advertisement on the tri-state area's Hot 97 radio station for New York City Public School teachers. Within one week of hearing the advertisement, I applied, interviewed, and started my journey as a teacher for students with disabilities at Franklin K. Lane High School in Cypress Hills, Brooklyn in September 2000.

I wonder if the teaching job was my equivalent of a rebound relationship. You know, the action that some of us take when a relationship that we were so invested in emotionally, physically, and mentally does not work out, so we jump head-first into something new. Was my immediate desire to teach, although I planned to do so eventually, my way of seeking out the other possibility to find and commit to what I genuinely loved? Rebound or not, I found love in September 2000 and have been in love ever since.

It was there in the classroom that I battled through the recent pain of feeling like a failure. It was also in the classroom where I watched feelings of despair dissipate and found opportunities for hope every day. Back then when I arrived at work, every classroom interaction with my students lifted me. I regularly felt great reward when they would achieve challenging academic, social and behavioral outcomes. In hindsight, I realize that it is amazing how a failure can serve as the catalyst to discover our purpose and our WHY. After seven years as a special education teacher in New York and Baltimore City, I was called to serve as a principal. At that time, I did not have the professional maturity, nor was I self-actualized enough to embrace the tenets of an empathetic leader. However, actual experiences as a principal and district leader changed me. Today, I ground my work and my coaching approaches in a radical pursuit of equity and empathy as a direct result of what I learned in those early years.

While noble, the road has not always been easy. My approach to educational leadership and community activism over the years has created uneasiness in many peers, colleagues, direct reports, and supervisors alike. I am aware that I have intentionally and unintentionally created disruption and disequilibrium in many schools and districts where reluctance to see the necessity for an intentional approach that serves ALL students ALL teachers get in the way. However, this relentless focus on everyone is only obtained through radical empathy in leadership. A radically empathetic and equity focused orientation will inevitably create discomfort, disagreements, disdain, and if not managed well, distraction from the work at hand. The work of improving and scaling outcomes for all students, with an increased focus on doing so for Black students, as well as other students of color requires a shift in more than just additional resources. District and school leaders need to focus on the creation of a critical consciousness and culturally proficient competencies in practitioners. It requires actions that are not just focused on inputs such as surface level changes in the schoolhouse. It requires uplifting the conversations about race, racial outcomes, disproportionality, and oppression with the same vigor and commitment as the conversations about other academic and technical outputs. In fact, these outputs necessitate disrupting and dissolving systems of inequality. The protocols and structures that have resulted in the marginal success of the K-12 institutions in the U.S. cannot come at the expense of Black students and other students of color.

The work of scaling and improving outcomes for all students requires bringing along adults of every orientation and historically marginalized groups (LGBTQ, Native Americans, Students With Disabilities, Women, African Americans, LatinX), but not at the risk of diminishing the importance of, or diluting the much needed discussions about race. Essentially, if we are serious about changing the landscape of the current education system that now serves over 53 million students with more than 50% of those students being from underrepresented communities, we must embrace radical empathy in leadership.

Chapter 3.

The Case for Radical Empathy

Radical is being used as an adjective to mean far-reaching or thorough. The word implies advocating for a fundamental shift in something. Marrying "radical" to "empathy" is intentional. Empathy, unlike sympathy, is possessing the desire to understand someone by trying to understand how they think, what they feel, and how they believe. This level of understanding without the accompanying "radical" is in short supply. It is natural for people to focus on their own positions and what they think, feel, and believe whenever they are engaging with others. But what if we were thorough in our quest to understand other people? What if we fundamentally shift what it means to be empathetic? That is the case I am making.

Radical empathy is the relentless commitment to fundamentally change our orientation from judgmental to accepting. It is being deliberate about shifting from self-serving positions to ones of understanding the lived experience of others. Radical empathy is a visual display of a willingness of spirit to improve lives. The case for radical empathy in leadership has been made repeatedly in various forms. On the national level, we have witnessed the call for policy makers to spend time understanding their constituents' needs instead of voting for their personal political future. The hope has been that in understanding, the resulting laws and policies would cause more on-the-ground actions that support more people, more often.

Instead, what we have seen is many instances where public displays by professionals in service industries have made decisions that altered the lives of others because those decisions were devoid of a basic empathetic approach. Police officers have leaned into policing when the expectation should have been one of protecting and serving. Superintendents have made decisions to terminate instead of coaching and developing principals. Principals have terminated or transferred teachers when a commitment to understanding the needs of that school leader or teacher would have made a positive difference in the lives of the leader, teacher, and ultimately, students. Policy makers, who have had vastly different lived experiences from their constituents, vote on life altering decisions that negatively impacted those whom they served, simply because they seek to be understood, instead of seeking to understand.

There are numerous sources that echo the plight of Black students and other students of color in contemporary U.S. society in general, and this country's K-12 system in particular. The Aspen Institute shared that the way students are treated in school can trigger or ameliorate stereotype threat. Stereotype Threat occurs when people feel they are at risk of being stigmatized by assumptions that associate their social identity with undesirable characteristics. Students who have received societal or school-delivered messages implying that they are less capable of achieving as a function of race, ethnicity, language background, gender, economic status, or disability will often translate those views into negative self-perceptions. These negative perceptions reduce the confidence of students in their ability to achieve academically and socially. The call to action is for large doses of radical empathy in leadership to be bestowed on these students, as well as the adults who serve, and even those who deserve them.

Three factors speak to the sense of urgency that is needed for a radical empathetic and equity-focused approach to teaching and leading in K-12 education and beyond:

1. **Dropout Rate**: Given the disproportionate number of students of color who are pushed out of schools (every 26 seconds, 1 high school student drops out = 7,000 daily = 1.2 million each year; this includes 40% drop out rate for Black male students and 35% for Latino male students) and

denied opportunities to become college ready or exposed to excellent academic environments is evidence that our current political and educational landscape warrants such an approach.

2. **Demographic Shifts**: According to the National Center for Educational Statistics for the first time in the history of K-12 education, underrepresented students are now the majority who are enrolled representing 50.5% of those enrolled. These are the students who must grapple daily with academic content and environments that do not include their culture, heritage, or experiences into the daily practices.

3. **Silenced Black and Other Leaders of Color**: My experiences as Black education leader has resulted in my daily interactions with other adults of color who are politically and positionally powerful, being judged harshly and discouraged. The underrepresented adults, like the children, are also disparaged, marginalized, and criticized. This criticism is not because of qualifications, intellectual prowess, or abilities, but simply because of race and ethnicity. It speaks to the fact that our schools and educational arena has not

yet committed to structures that embrace and sustain the diverse linguistic and culturally different backgrounds of adults in the building either.

I intend to capture the experiences and reflections of teachers, school, and district leaders whose experiences mirror that of many of you who are deeply committed to making our system better for all students. I know that you struggle daily with fighting the pervasive systemic oppression, manipulative marginalization, and paucity of liberatory education that exists. I know too well that trying to replace it with a system that unapologetically addresses inequity and racialized outcomes is tough.

To be clear, my intention is not to inspire you to feel sorry for or sympathize with those who have been victimized by oppression and marginalization. However, **empathy** is not **sympathy**, nor feeling sorry for others. Instead, it is the willingness to understand what others are feeling, thinking, experiencing, and taking action to be helpful to them. My intention is to position you to help take action to change these bleak circumstances for ALL students and adults using radical empathy.

Essentially, **radically empathetic leadership** is your willingness to recognize and acknowledge that an unprecedented level of emotional turmoil and discomfort will be felt by both victims and perpetrators of systemic oppression and marginalization. However, the unapologetic push for an urgent disruption of the status-quo and the cultivating of relational trust across differences must occur. When it does it will be perceived as radical and not essential. However, it must be accomplished with the willingness to understand the other person's journey.

Chapter 4.

Are America's Schools Being Setup for Failure?

With President Obama's signing of Every Student Succeed Act (ESSA) on December 10, 2015, two of the key elements of this bipartisan measure is the relinquishing of control of education back to states and districts. In essence it moved education decision making away from the prescriptive nature of the No Child Left Behind Act (NCLB). Yes, this law was partially a response to the call on President Obama's administration, and many pedagogical theorists and practitioners to create a policy that really focused on preparing our students for success. The hope was that it would increase competitiveness of U.S. students amongst their peers around the world. Sounds great, however, I wondered how many states and districts are ready to assume total responsibility for the educational journey of our nation's most precious jewels, our children. Were we as a nation ready to regain our place of preeminence as the educational powerhouse we once were?

Nelson Madibá Mandela reminds us that "there can be no keener revelation of a society's soul than the way it treats its children." The truth is, although it appears that our lagging system of K-12 education and achievement performance ranking amongst the developed countries in the world is a recent phenomenon, this decline started more than a half century ago with the U.S.S.R.'s launch of Sputnik in October 1957. This launch precipitated the response around the urgency to create an education system that would prepare all of the nation's children for excellence. Although this was the beginning of presidential and federal educational policies, school and district leaders have continuously experienced their share of such policies impacting and influencing their work. These policies include President Johnson's 1965 Every Student Succeeds Act (ESEA), to President Reagan's 1989 Nation at Risk, President Clinton's Goals 2000, and President Bush's 2002 No Child Left Behind, with a reauthorization in 2004 by President Obama, and a subsequent change of heart if you may, with his signing of the ESSA on December 15, 2015.

One of the reasons we have experienced such significant failure is our unwillingness or inability to approach school reform using a systemic and scientific inquiry-based approach. Constantly changing education policy, most of which should remain in the annals of the ivory tower and schools of education will not revolutionize our approach and achieve the K-12 and post-secondary educational and achievement outcomes that we seek. With the expectation that there will likely be a change and different direction every four years because of our electoral system and governmental politics, it's no wonder that some of our school and district leaders' decision making sometimes mirrors constant adoptions of "flavor of the week" adaptations. It is the direct result of knowing that at any moment, a directive from an ideologue can change the course of any well-intentioned strategic plan.

For those who are not conversant with the workings and daily expectations of United States' school leaders, our daily instructional and operational tasks are monumental to say the least. From the time a CEO, superintendent, principal, assistant principal, or teacher's feet hit the floor in the wee hours of the morning, we are faced with at least 500 decisions that day. In spite of these challenges, these education leaders are expected to navigate the monstrosities of the existing and inequitable bureaucracies that are associated with our K-12 education system:

- parents who need a lot of love (tough and other)

- staff who are relying on us for guidance and support

- students whose academic deficits, social emotional needs and challenges, and the need for parental guidance must be prioritized.

America's school leaders' ability to balance the dichotomous relationship between technical and adaptive decision making is perceived as equal to and in some instances superior to that of their counterparts in other developed countries. Yet our student's (particularly Black students, other students of color and other marginalized groups) academic performance is not reflective of such exemplary leadership.

It is clear that we have the largest number of schools of education, tier 1 research universities, and a voluminous existence of archives and libraries of dissertations and thesis providing theories and guidance in educational theories for educators at every level. It may surprise you to know that a thorough examination of these resources will reveal that amongst this existing research from the past 50 years, there is a paucity of research and guidance for educators to lead and teach from a lens that is focused on equity and empathy. All the studying is not changing the on-the-ground outcomes.

Educator preparation programs and tier 1 universities in the U.S. do not prepare our educators for the harsh realities of the work; realities that educators in other countries do not face. It is common knowledge amongst educators in America's

K-12 arena that principals and teachers are assaulted physically and verbally daily, and sometimes threatened personally, professionally, and emotionally in ways that are inconceivable to the non-K-12 practitioner or proletariat. In spite of such abuse and on-the-job trauma that school leader's experience, most of them still lead like lives depend on it.

Having awareness of the current state of the educational landscape where the most committed public servants toil for 180 days evokes many questions. One such question is, "Why do teachers, related service providers and school leaders demonstrate such resilience by not taking such abuse personally? Another question is why, in spite of such abuse, their commitment to support the students and adults who perpetuate that abuse is unwavering? These questions are even more perplexing if you consider that there are other professions that have zero tolerance for verbal berating and threats or any of the aforementioned abuses that are rampant in the K-12 education arena.

For 20 years I have observed our declining and ineffective educational policy structures, the only constants are the dedicated and highly effective school leaders, teachers, and staff. This group of professionals show up each day and deliver to our nation's children regardless of who is in the White House, Governor's mansion, Mayor's house, or district office. As the result of my observations, interactions, and discussions with principals, assistant principals, other school level leaders, and teachers in more than 60 school districts, I am convinced that they are the proverbial glue that holds the fledgling public education system in place.

The issue of educational failure does not rest with our school leaders. Although a principal can impact as much as 25% of academic increase of students, and 50% of the school's climate and culture, they sometimes are not given the respect that they have earned and deserve. Given the level of impact that school leaders and their teams have on the educational outcomes of students, I have a few wonderings and lots of questions. Here are some of my questions:

- Can our education system regain the reputation of being a place where students in grades K-12 get access to a sound education for ALL?

- What would happen if those of us who are in positions of policy and district leadership inculcate the belief that we work for schools and principals, and on behalf of children; and it is not the other way around?

- Have we exhausted the amount of educational and pedagogical theory, discussions, and forums about how to improve our systems at scale?

- Is it time that we embark upon a deep dive into practical applications by tapping the credibility of successful practitioners (teachers and principals) who have a record of positively impacting student achievement?

- As district leaders, will we get immediate traction around increased student achievement and improved teacher practice and morale if our daily actions echo the belief that we work for schools and they do not work for us?

- Can we stop the practice of subjecting school leaders to "professional development" that is facilitated by individuals who have no leadership, especially school leadership experience or pertinent credibility?

The ranking system via the Program for International Student Assessment (PISA) places U.S. Education reading at 28th and math at 29th amongst the developed countries in the world. However, this is not in any way an indication of the quality of leadership that exists within the schools in this country. An examination of the conditions under which our principal and their senior leadership teams lead, the circumstances that they face daily, and the policies and bureaucratic entanglements that they strategically navigate daily are all indications of the amazing cadre of school principals, assistant principals, and deans.

I respectfully submit that although there is tremendous value in exploring and implementing new ideas and initiatives, there are too many that were superfluous. Curricula changes every year, shifting from small schools to community schools, to schools without walls, to charter schools, to whole school reform, to school within a school. Then there was standards-based grading, and laxed assessment requirements, and increased accountability for testing, expeditionary learning, and many others.

Yes, there was some value added in some of those movements and initiatives. The issue is the fact that there has never been any true investment in real school leader development at scale. The best attempts to date have been the New Leaders for New Schools (New Leaders) principal preparation program, the 2015 Wallace Foundation and Washington University's Principal Supervisor Standards report, and maybe one or two other attempts. The New Leaders data echoes that they have had a strong impact on changing the educational landscape via exemplary and culturally competent leadership, and the expected trickle-down impact on teacher development and student achievement. Let me be clear, the panacea rests in truly investing in, and developing a solid cadre of school leaders who can inspire, develop, and motivate teachers and students. We need school leaders who lead from an orientation that is empathetic. School leaders in the United States K-12 education system are amongst the most committed, dedicated, and selfless professionals around. There are still too many instances whereby they are not treated as the consummate professionals that they are. While I think they are doing an excellent job, one area of growth is aligning the technical aspects of the work to a relentless focus on empathy.

Shane's Story

The role of an educator, regardless of position can be incredibly challenging and equally as rewarding. It is said that the average life expectancy in the role as principal is 2-4 years. Shane was in his second year as principal of Central Valley High School. Perusing his resume, almost anyone would be impressed. He had completed graduate studies at some of the nation's most prestigious universities, served as an outstanding teacher, and moved up through the ranks to become a high school principal. From all indications and a review of his first year in the role, he and his team experienced many successes but had some areas where they needed to get better. Shane's immediate supervisor was his superintendent, Tony. Unfortunately, Tony's inclination to pay attention to Shane's deficits rather than his strengths was not helpful to Shane. Like many principal supervisors, Tony only cared about student achievement, teacher satisfaction and morale, safety, and other student outcomes. All of his priorities were important, but not necessarily aligned with Shanes' professional development and personal needs. Ultimately, at the end of his second year, Shane was removed from his position under the guise that he failed as a principal and was not a good fit.

The Necessary Shift Toward Radical Empathy

Shane would have benefitted from Tony's actions that should have included:

1. Asking Shane what his goals were, what was getting in the way of achieving those goals, and what he needed from Tony.

2. Tony should have provided Shane with clarity of expectations but emphasized to Shane that he was willing to exhaust every attempt at supporting him to achieve his goals.

3. While clarifying for Shane that he will be held accountable for the agreed upon outcomes, that he was responsible for seeking out proof points or exemplars from schools and leaders who are doing similar work in other schools.

Tony's radically empathetic approach to coaching Shane should strike a balance of shared accountability and targeted, differentiated support. Although America continues to fall on the list of exemplary K-12 education in the world, it is not because of the adults that serve them. Instead, the system requires both radical empathy and radical reform. Our leaders deserve the best resources and support so that education is not a fleeting career for brilliant professionals, but noble pursuit where people are prioritized over politics, and humanity is elevated over processes and outcomes.

Chapter 5.

The Empathetic and Compassionate Leader's Framework

Who is the leader residing inside of you? Not the one who showed up to the interview and regurgitated all of the buzz-words or pleasant-sounding educational rhetoric of the day to impress the often less than qualified interviewer or interview panel. Who are you at the core of your philosophy on life and leadership? Who are you when your subordinates and direct reports are not around? In 2016 the Wall Street Journal featured an article titled, "*The Perils of Empathy*" written by Paul Bloom in which we are reminded that while empathy often helps us do what's right, it sometimes motivates us to do what's wrong. Empathy distorts our judgement." Although I do not know Paul Bloom, my research knowledge and experience with empathetic and compassionate leadership inspired my rebuttal. In order to grasp the context and so that you have a different perspective, I encourage you to read the articles and other publications in the issue of the Wall Street Journal.

This journal article raised my eyebrows with the first para-graph. In the initial paragraph, the author confused empathy with sympathy. This error is understandable because this is a common mistake in academia and other professional arenas. The author also stated that trying to feel the pain of others (sympathy) is a bad idea. On the contrary, it should be noted that empathy is the understanding of another. The author's stance throughout this article gives the impression that in order to survive the politics of leadership, you must be heartless as a leader. Essentially, the article is thought provoking but limited on its attempt at effective generalizations.

Yes, the arena of K-12 education is riddled with aspects of policy and politics. However, built into every policy and political decision are children and people who are committed to alleviating the struggles and improving the trajectory of those children. There are children at the ends of these data points and educators cannot ignore the pain of students. Lacking empathy is essentially harnessing an unwillingness to understand the pain, failure, and suffering of others. Devoid of empathy, it is impossible to be willing to take action to alleviate pain, failure, and suffering. The article is a sobering reminder that there is a lack of understanding the necessity of empathy in our everyday actions. As it relates to our work, I believe that there is an empathy deficit amongst the cadre of district and school leaders in urban, suburban, and rural school districts alike. People often think that this issue is an urban school district issue alone. It is not. Evaluate the performance outcomes of underrepresented students in any district and you will notice a concerning pattern - the children who need the most help get the least amount of empathy.

The good news is that empathetic and compassionate leadership are competencies that can be shared and developed through capacity building efforts. In fact, I have tremendous hope for our school districts, as well as a strongly reinforced belief that a nation-wide shift in our leadership requirements and practices to include empathetic leadership as a necessary competency is possible. We have to remember that organizational policy and politics are not always about elevating the best interest of people. They are often ivory-tower conceptualizations that rarely take into account the human element and the potential impact on people's lives.

Conversely, teaching and leading in high need, under supported, and underserved communities is a people-focused pursuit. Any idea that "perverse moral mathematics" whereby people in their cognitive processing have to prioritize who and when to express, and even lead with empathy is wrong. It would behoove us to implement a practice in any school district to find a way to screen candidates who apply for leadership positions for empathy and compassion leadership proclivity as essential school leadership competencies.

Unlike politics, in K-12 education we cannot be subjective about how we share or dish out empathy. In spite of ideological and philosophical differences, embracing empathy in education or any other arena should be as necessary as oxygen. Every person, every student, and every teacher deserves an unlimited supply, but this must be balanced with a strong state of accountability (when one exhausts their supply of empathy). This idea that suggests that "when we set empathy aside, we make better policy" is problematic in isolation. While I certainly agree that when I am tasked with making decisions that impact a larger group, objectivity is critical, this does not mean that I set empathy aside. The inherent issue with this sentiment is the fact that there are gaps between policy and people, policy and implementation, and policy and reality.

Too often policy makers huddle in settings with just a snippet of the reality of the subjects, needs, and people that their policy and plan will affect, particularly the emotional or cognitive state of those impacted. **Cognitive empathy** as defined by what the psychology community refers to our ability to recognize the emotional state of another person. Interestingly enough, the research does not discuss what steps should be taken to change or impact that state.

I am regularly intrigued when leaders are discouraged from focusing on empathy and compassion as a necessary leadership or organizational approach. Unlike these rigid theoretical approaches, I am committed to publish contrary works that marry research and theory with the practitioners' insights to support the overwhelmingly positive impact of empathy and compassion. In the meantime, I strongly encourage school leaders to embrace an empathetic approach more often than not.

As you try to inspire change through an empathetic and culturally responsive approach, consider the human being at the other end of the policy, numbers, or other data points. This decision will likely increase your investment and that of your team in an empathy-based goal achievement culture. For educators, remember that at the end of every data point are children.

Robert's Story

Do you even know my name?

This was the question Chloe posed to her principal during parent - teacher night. Feeling the embarrassment of being put on the spot, Robert realized that as principal of this school, he was standing face to face with a student who was a part of a nuclear family, on the honor roll, never had any discipline infractions, and by most standards, a model student. Chloe asked her questions about five minutes into a conversation that Robert was having with her parents about her. A conversation where he used all of the generalizations such as expressions of gratitude for them being there, how great a student she was, discussing the challenges that the school faced that year, and celebrating all of his amazing teachers and the outstanding work of the community with regards to partnerships. Chloe's question, while catching him off guard, would eventually change his leadership orientation. In response to Chloe's question in front of her parents on that day, he reluctantly admitted that he did not know her name. She was a junior and had been at the school for three years.

Robert realized that during his tenure as a principal, he had spent an inordinate amount of time focused on the data rather than students at the end of each point. While this is an excellent practice, it was troubling to him that he, like many school leaders, had focused on the students who were highflyers to the principals or dean's office. Students who were often academically inclined, complied with the student code of conduct, and remained focused on their future goals in traditional ways went under the radar of leaders like Robert. He was the first to admit during our conversation that the interaction with Chloe and her parents changed how he served students for years to come. Not only did he increase his own commitment to ensure that he knew the names of every student, or introduced himself to them at least once in any given school year, he expected that every adult in the building made this a priority.

The Necessary Shift Toward Radical Empathy

Chloe, and every student like her, needs their teachers and school leaders to go above and beyond to ensure that they are seen, heard, and feel supported. This means that every student should be paired with an adult in the building. The expectation should be that the assigned adult will commit to establishing authentic relationships with the students. There should be some intentionality with the matching of students and adults. This matching includes connecting students and adults when they have had very different lived experiences and also sometimes when their lives are quite similar. Ultimately, we have found that these relationships blossom into perpetual and life-long friendships. Making this shift is an example of demonstrating radical empathy.

Recently I was on a return flight from Washington D.C. to Oakland, California, returning home after conducting business related to education policy on Capitol Hill. As I stood in line waiting to check my bag, a gentleman approached me with vigor and in a vociferous manner called out my name. As he got closer, I recognized his face and realized that while I remembered him as a student, he now stood about three inches taller than me. With tears in his eyes, simultaneously he embraced me and shook my hand. He stepped back after about 20 seconds and said, "Thank you for saving my life. Thank you for giving me a chance to get better." He then asked me if I remembered telling him and his mother that he needed to have his own necktie the next day or he would not be allowed into the school. He reminded me that I took him to the office and gave him a tie. With tears still in his eyes he said, "I better get back to my desk at the airlines before you have me crying in front of these people." He walked away and then I remembered his name; Victor. Subsequently we found each other on social media and today we are in touch frequently.

Consider being more deliberate about creating the same kinds of relationship pairings between children and adults in your buildings. But know that too often our focus is on the children alone. We have to remember that the teachers, staff members and other adults would benefit from also having intentional relationships with coworkers they wouldn't naturally form bonds with.

Chapter 6.

Embracing the New Shift to Radical Empathy

Do As I Do

"Do as I say and not as I do!"

Clearly, we may not say this in our roles as teachers, school, and district leaders. However, our actions in many instances convey and perpetuate this universal adage. As principals we expect our teachers to connect with their students on a level that goes deeper than their cognitive capacity and ability to achieve at unprecedented academic levels. In our weekly staff meetings, we remind teachers that if students know that you care, they will perform for you. Similarly, we encourage senior and executive leaders such as C suite occupants such as superintendents and assistant superintendents to model what servant, supportive, and exemplary leadership of principals mean. This often includes understanding that many of our nation's principals are operating from the paradigm of being administrators and managers of complex institutions called schools. The management or administrator's paradigm focuses more on the daily operational and highly technical aspect of the buildings, which often neglects the real mission of the school or district. In most instances, the mission of schools and school districts is anchored in providing educational opportunities for the students they serve. Conversely, the new paradigm is one that highlights the necessity for principals to pivot their way towards the work to serve as instructional leaders inevitably has a learning curve, and therefore requires superintendents, assistant superintendents, and other principal supervisors to navigate such learning curves through an empathetic orientation. One resource that is helpful to support school and district leaders in this endeavor came in 2015. That year, the Wallace Foundation and Washington University produced a report titled, *"Model Principal Supervisor Professional Standards."* In this report, the researchers indicated that as a part of their long-term commitment to the development and sharing of knowledge, insights, and ideas to improve education leadership, having strong principal supervisory standards is a game changer for school leaders. Their arrival at eight research-based standards was intended to ultimately assist principals and assistant principals to accelerate improvement of student learning.

The Wallace Foundation research and standards reminds us that although principals are under much scrutiny now more than ever to be instructional leaders (new paradigm), and transform the schools they lead, they are not prepared to do so. This needed improvement requires those who supervise principals to focus less on the evaluative aspect of such supervision and increase coaching and support through an empathetic orientation. Such an orientation does not mean laxed accountability, but a focus on shared accountability for teacher improvement and student outcomes.

My recent polling of school leaders in more than 57 schools and districts found that 93% of them did not practice what they preached in meetings, shared expectations, and public requests. It is not that these professionals did not want to lead by example, in many instances, they were not equipped to do so because of the lack of focus on the people and more on the product. The bureaucratic and pre-historic nature of many school systems keeps them focusing on the old paradigm, but expect the leaders to pivot to the new. The new paradigm requires supervisors to make authentic connections with those who they lead. This skill set could benefit from targeted and differentiated professional development on leading with empathy.

Decide today to lead by example from an empathetic orientation:

- What ways can you expect yourself and others to connect with staff members on a deeper level that goes beyond their skill, talent and ability?

- How do you ensure that everyone on your staff knows that you care so that they will perform for you?

"If I commit to leading with compassion, will I be seen as weak?" "Does this mean that I cannot hold people accountable?" "Is this leadership stance a reflection of being decision-averse?" "Can I correct or terminate an ineffective employee with empathy and compassion?"

These are a few questions I have fielded during the past few years while sharing my work from *The Power of Seven Second-Chances* and leading sessions around teaching and leading with empathy and compassion. These questions inspire me to reflect on my own initial questions about the importance leading with empathy and compassion. I posed these questions:

1. Does a commitment to leading with empathy cost me anything?

2. Does a commitment to lead with empathy make me a weak leader?

3. Does a commitment to empathy get in the way of attaining the desired outcomes and achieving the bottom line?

4. Does my commitment to lead with empathy benefit those who I serve and lead?

In response to my questioning, a good friend reminded me that Jesus, Gandhi, and Buddha all taught these ideas prior to any contemporary leaders who attempt to coin empathetic leadership concepts as their own. It is my goal to apply centuries-old teaching to educational leadership and practice. With that, I am simply submitting that it is prudent to understand the situations and circumstances of those you are teaching and leading. I am also suggesting that you anchor your leadership approach in this knowledge because you are making critical student and personnel decisions every day.

Leading from a place of empathy and compassion will not require a 360 degree change in leadership style or a complete dismantling of your leadership philosophy. It *will* require a simple pivot towards recognizing that people are worth more to organizations than their cognitive capacity or ability to contribute to the bottom line. Although I have spent more than a decade engaging in this practice, I am still growing to adopt and fully embrace this philosophy consistently in my own leadership journey. What is clear to me is that when all else fails, school leaders can always find comfort in an empathetic leadership and teaching stance. A stance where they prioritize the physical, socio-emotional, and mental health and well-being of the people they are tasked with leading.

Getting Started

Investing and pushing teachers and school leaders to embrace teaching and leading with empathy and compassion to transform classrooms all started with my observation of the disparate treatment of neophyte teachers, underrepresented students, and students with disabilities. While teaching and leading with empathy and compassion has little to do with tenure, race and class, or ability, it is anchored in outcomes that catapult academic achievement (as measured by any standardized assessment). So where should you begin?

As a middle and high school principal for almost decade, I committed to leading with empathy and compassion. Among the ways that this commitment manifested itself was through my reminders to the teachers and staff to engage in two daily **non-negotiable practices:**

1. Introduce themselves to at least one student whose name they did not know, or who they did not teach directly. Over time, intentionally establish a positive relationship with that student.

2. Compliment at least one student or colleague daily. Recognizing that it may be the only positive sentiment that person hears that day. Do not miss the opportunity to be the server of it.

Many people think that a compassionate and empathetic approach is time-consuming, the antithesis of strong leadership, and delays the achievement of strong outcomes. However, I often push them to consider that there is an incredible value-add when principals have a thorough understanding of the existence of their teachers and staff beyond what is written on the resume. Similarly, when teachers are familiar with every student on their caseload, this can result in the cultivation of authentic, reciprocal relationships that increase student investment in their educational outcomes. As an adult, think of what makes you feel valued as a person, not as a professional. Similarly, think of what will make your students or direct reports feel valued as individuals. Viewing your staff members as students or as mere subjects who are a part of your evidence for the next data meeting is not likely going to result in the outcomes you desire.

Michael's Story

In his role as assistant principal of a large urban high school, Michael knew that the work ahead would be challenging. He had assumed the role two years prior and noticed one of the immediate challenges was the high suspension rates. After reviewing the data, he realized the need to pivot. In his role, Michael was responsible for student discipline which meant any violations of the student's code of conduct was referred to him. As a part of his theory of action, Michael had a zero-tolerance policy for students and assigned out of school suspensions (OSS) for 100% of students who had such violations. A conversation with his coach, a district officer leader resulted in the two of them conducting an analysis of the trend data for the past three years. The analysis revealed that there was a disproportionate number of OSS to certain groups of students.

The students who were impacted disproportionately included students with disabilities, English Language Learners, and African American students. Michael was focused on "cleaning up" the school's culture which he stated was being influenced by the students who are always disrupting instruction, arriving at school late, not completing their assignments, and violating the students code of conduct. In reflection, Michael stated that he made decisions to remove students from school who were sometimes not coming to school, essentially giving them what they wanted. Similarly, he discovered that the students who were suspended from school were those who could have benefited more from being in school. Suspending the students who were not doing well was counterproductive to the school's mission of providing a quality education to all students. Michael realized that the school's 15% annual drop-out rate included 75% of those students who were frequent flyers in the out of school suspension group. This was a direct result of his zero-tolerance approach versus an empathetic one.

The Necessary Shift Toward Radical Empathy

Michael and any school or district leader should pivot towards a radically empathetic approach by asking a series of questions to gain an understanding of the underlying cause of the student's code of conduct infractions. Essentially, a root cause analysis of sorts. The seven questions that Michael's coach encouraged him to ask prior to suspending any student were:

1. What's the child's living situation? Who lives with them? This gives insights into the student's home life.

2. Is this a typical violation by this student?

3. What are the student's goals for themselves for the school year? Does the student have goals? Are they written? Who is assisting them with remaining focused on these goals?

4. Does the student have a personal or mentoring relationship with an adult in the school? These relationships usually increase their love for being in school, and doing what is right for the adults with whom they have a positive relationship. Students, adolescents will not have positive

relationships and like every adult in their school building. Having at least one such relationship is helpful.

5. What was the student's disposition and academic inclination like prior to their arrival at that school? Prior to the current grade? Understanding the student's journey is a helpful guide as a teacher or school administrator makes decisions that will impact a student's life.

6. Does the student have an Individualized Education Plan (IEP) or other special needs? Understanding this will provide insights into any mitigating factors that may have resulted in the student's violation of the code of conduct.

7. What are alternative actions that the administrator can take, or what are alternatives to out of school suspension that will ultimately help the student?

As a result of the pivot to a radically empathetic approach of prioritizing persons over processes and policies, Michael and his team of teachers saw a 60% reduction in their out of school suspension data, whenever they had a potential conflict with peers, students were more inclined to seek out the guidance of adults with whom they had cultivated positive relationships, and many parents shared feedback with the school's team that they noticed the changes in their children. Michael shared that the most compelling and rewarding data point for his school's team is that they were able to locate and convince 41 of the 60 12th graders who had dropped out of school during the past two years. Of those students, 30 of them graduated from high school that year and the remaining 11 were enrolled in credit recovery programs en route to graduation. Radical empathy requires intentional disruption to systems that are perpetuating the status-quo but not advancing the quality of life of people.

Chapter 7.

Are Some Educators Selectively Empathetic and Compassionate?

In a recent study conducted, it was uncovered that 75% of school leaders and teachers surveyed do not consistently practice empathy and compassion in leadership. However, these same leaders expect that empathy and compassion will translate to the children in our schools. I have often wondered about my colleagues who pretend to exhibit empathetic leadership but are committed to ridiculing, criticizing, and emasculating their peers and colleagues who are not a part of their privileged, racial, cultural, or socio-economic circle. What is striking is that they spend between 20-60 hours per week working in school and district together with the same people, fighting the same challenges. They are known to be critical of these individuals, usually Black and Hispanic, who are immensely qualified, dedicated, loyal, and committed to serving students. Yet, these critics profess to love and care about the students and parents who are the mirror images of the very colleagues who they ridicule, castigate, and undermine. The truth is, such displays are the antithesis of empathetic and compassionate teaching and leadership.

The First Seven Leader Commitments

During my tenure as a school leader, two groups of teachers who have benefitted from my own displays of radical empathy are first year teachers, and those who became teachers thought alternative teacher preparation programs such as Teach for America (TFA). First year teachers often find that the theoretical exposure to pedagogy and content knowledge are only but a few of the critical resources that can help them to be successful. The emotional commitment required of them based on their investment into the lives of their students can become a heavy burden. This emotional toll coupled with the steep learning curve of balancing lesson planning, with differentiated lesson delivery, building authentic relationships with students and their families, and becoming culturally proficient quickly leads to much frustration.

Similarly, I reference TFA teachers because this group more than any has benefitted from a radically empathic orientation of mine and many of my colleagues who served as principals. The TFA program is the most successful teacher alternative preparation program that has placed hundreds of thousands of teachers in urban schools throughout the United States. A significant number of teachers who matriculate through this program have had very different lived experiences from the students they signed up to teach. In most cases, they have little to no experience with the communities where the schools are located. Their average tenure, especially at the schools where they are placed, is two years.

As a principal, I have had as much as 65% of my cadre of teachers be TFA corps members, and they have been tremendously impactful on student outcomes. I have also seen retention rates that far exceeded the two-year norm. I posit that the reason for those successes is my commitment to encouraging my leadership teams, as well as my principal peers to provide multiple opportunities for development, support, and improvement to TFA and first year teachers.

Additionally, in the true fashion of radical empathy, together we modeled the willingness to be empathetic to TFA teachers, who in turn were expected to do the same for the students they taught.

Commitment One: Relentless Belief in Students

Regardless of their academic, behavioral, or social deficits, demonstrate culturally competent leadership by recognizing the need for, and exercise intentionality around building and supporting healthy adult teams and healthy children. Bryan Stevenson in his book *"Just Mercy"* reminds us that people are better than their worst mistakes. In many instances, students and adults have had lived experiences that do not show them in a positive light. Empathetic leaders commit to seeing the potential in people and over-index on such potential versus their past.

Commitment Two: Growth Mindset

For yourself and others in the organization, believe that everyone can continuously grow, invest in, and steadily execute the mission and vision of the organization. Inevitably, people will have a learning curve when they are new to a team or organization. Consider the fact that if an individual(s) successfully navigated the recruitment, interview, and hiring process to get on the team, surely, they can learn the skills that are needed to be successful in their roles, and contribute to the bottom line. Empathetic leaders believe that people can, instead of thinking that they cannot.

Commitment Three: Courageous and Disruptive Leadership

Courageous and disruptive leadership is an exercise of leadership where the practitioner intentionally and continuously disrupts the status-quo to ensure the benefit to the masses; but does so within the parameters of what is legal, ethical, and moral. Radical empathy sometimes requires leaders to challenge the mental models of those around them, including those in positions of authority and influence. The ultimate goal of such an orientation is to ensure that the desired outcome of their actions benefits people, and prioritizes people over processes and protocols.

Commitment Four: Reflective

Engages in the re-examination of my own practices, dispositions, and biases with the goal of becoming more efficient and effective for daily operational excellence. The process of questioning one's decisions and thought processes in a positive way can provide great insights into future decisions and actions. When utilizing an operation plan that drives the daily operational and administrative decisions, one should have a healthy appetite to tweak and adjust as often as necessary. For example, the student entry practices, the scheduled timing and grade level breakdown for lunches and recess are all areas that allow for much end of day and end of week reflections, subsequently resulting in adjustments and changes.

Commitment Five: Prioritize Development

By creating sustainable systems that are evidenced-based with a track record of excellent outcomes when implemented, leaders should prioritize the capacity building and professional development of their peers and direct reports. Such approach to prioritizing development should be grounded in a targeted and differentiated approach that meets the needs of all. It is incumbent upon leaders and supervisors to create a culture that is not risk-averse. One hundred percent of teammates should believe that if they make mistakes or fall short of a goal, they are in an environment that will afford them the opportunity to correct the mistake, get better at the work, or get another shot at achieving the goal.

Commitment Six:
Create Equal and Equitable Practices

Recognizes that inequity is pervasive in education. It is one of the biggest impediments which prevent ALL children from receiving the appropriate resources to change their trajectory. Similarly, inequitable practices marginalize and prevent some adults from optimizing their performance and potential. Leaders should be intentional about treating everyone on their team equally, ensuring that there is fairness in their practices and policies (equality). Additionally, leaders should have the wherewithal to recognize the instances where some individuals and groups of people ought to be given more or additional support because of the innate systems and structures that had given them an unearned disadvantage (equity). The radically empathetic leader is committed to both equality and equity for teammates and students.

Commitment Seven: Data Driven

All practices are steeped in the use of multiple data sets (qualitative, quantitative, empirical), and all decisions are anchored in the analysis and interpretation of such data. The radically empathetic leader utilizes a multifactorial approach to data-driven decision making. This includes a relentless consistency to anchor 100% of decisions in a protocol that allows for objectivity and equity. For example, every decision, particularly those that have a level of complexity should be grounded in three questions:

1. What is the analytics and data available?

2. What is the commitment to equity and who will the decision impact?

3. Who is responsible for driving the communication machine after the data decision is finalized?

Second Seven Leader Commitments

Second Commitment One: Encourage Accountability

Practices empathetic and compassionate leadership, own the team's failure and growth, but celebrate/credit staff members for team/organization success and goal achievement. Radically empathetic leaders who encourage accountability ground such encouragement in shared accountability. One tactical approach to activating this is to make each teammate's objectives and the key actions and results aligned to these visible and accessible to other members of the team, and develop a culture where these are shared at bi-weekly or monthly intervals as necessary.

Second Commitment Two: Encourage Ownership

Practices shared accountability by not letting under performers off the hook, while intentionally discouraging high performers/achievers from becoming professionally aloof, and reiterating that every member of the team regardless of hierarchical position is equally as valuable. This is difficult to do if there is a culture of unequal or inequitable treatment of teammates outside of the C suite or executive team, based on where they fall on the hierarchy. When sharing the importance of ownership, this speaks to the teammate's investment in the achievement of the goals and desired outcomes of the team. With regards to the shared accountability, the expectation is for teammates to accept the responsibility for the failures or underperformance of each other, and anchor their approach in the adage; "a chain is as strong as its weakest link."

Second Commitment Three: Flexible Performance Management

Publicly praises and privately corrects colleagues for ineffective practice/underperformance. Inevitably, some teammates will fall short of achieving their goals or miss deadlines. While there should not be a culture that tolerates mediocrity, the radically empathetic leader asks a series of questions of teammates who are displaying mediocrity to assist them to achieve their goals. One example is for the supervisor to set performance goals that are also aligned to bi-weekly coaching and check-in conversations with the coachee or direct report. These conversations should always end with a clear way forward for the person being coached.

Second Commitment Four: Resilient Development Practices

Is willing to exhaust efforts at building capacity and correcting performance deficits. The radically empathetic leader is thoughtful, understands that mediocrity in any teammate impedes goal attainment, but does not resort to evaluation and termination as a first response. Targeted and focused opportunities to improve the skill set of direct reports and teammates are a priority. One tactical approach is to ensure that the professional development opportunities that are being made available to the teammates are not generalized to all, but more specific to their current roles and development goals.

Second Commitment Five: Promote Confidence

Empowers, encourages, and uplifts colleagues in an effortless manner. Recognizes when teammates are not exhibiting self-assuredness and confidence in their assigned roles, and commits to personally assist, or lead them to resources that will result in improved and increased confidence. The consistent public praising of teammates in written communication that includes the rest of the team and expressing gratitude for their work in staff and team meetings.

Second Commitment Six: Demonstrate Compassion

If there is ever a time that warrants the correction, or if necessary, chastising teammates, it is done in a manner that will not strip away one's dignity, but it occurs in a manner that highlights a commitment to shared accountability and offers opportunities for the struggling teammate to get better. While radical empathy demonstrates understanding of the challenge that the person needs or is trying to overcome, the demonstration of compassion is the verb or action alignment to assist them in doing so. This can be done through minimizing the corrective action against someone for errors while in public meetings, by using euphemistic terms such as "that's one perspective for us to consider." "Why don't we table this and explore or unpack this further in a smaller meeting." This allows the leader/supervisor to correct privately but do so expeditiously.

Second Commitment Seven: People First

Recognizes that people truly matter; my daily actions and leadership stances are a clear indicator that I believe this. People will believe that you think they really matter based on your daily actions and interactions with them in public and in private. Are you consistent with your praising, celebrating, correcting, coaching, and when necessary, evaluating? One tactical approach is to be more committed to pausing to receive a response when you ask someone how they are doing. Instead of treating it as an obligatory exchange of pleasantry, you should demonstrate a genuine interest in their response, and if necessary, do something to alleviate a negative response. For instance, what happens if you see Tom first thing in the morning at work and the exchange goes like this: "Good morning Tom, how are you?" Tom's response, "Nicole, thanks for asking. I am not feeling well. My wife has surgery tomorrow, I have to euthanize my dog, and I am feeling out of it." This is not an instance where your next response is; "well, have a great day Tom." A radically empathetic orientation will have you be an ear for Tom or find a resource that can be helpful.

First 7 Leadership Commitments	Second 7 Leadership Commitments
Relentless Belief in Students	Encourage Accountability
Growth Mindset	Encourage Ownership
Encourage Courageous and Disruptive Leadership	Embrace Flexible Performance Management
Utilize Reflective Practice	Employ Resilient Development Practices
Prioritize Development	Promote Confidence
Create Equitable Practices	Demonstrate Compassion
Be Data Driven	Put People First

The difference between the first seven commitments and the second seven commitments is to prioritize people and their needs versus practices and procedures. Many times, school leaders juxtapose the First 7 and Second 7 leadership commitments but still over index on the more technical focus on processes and policies, and not prioritize the needs of people. Most leaders believe that it is impossible to embrace both the First 7 and the Second 7 set of commitments simultaneously. The thinking and misconception are that if you eagerly practice the first seven, embracing the second seven will impede progress. I invite you to think about what you could accomplish in your schools and districts if you adopt both and become great at practicing them. Sometimes the limitations are only in our minds.

Kala's Story

Serving in the role of a school district leader truly epitomizes the adage, "the higher you go, the harder it is to breathe." Kala reminded the group of school leaders who she was tasked with leading that "leaders are signal senders," and a leader should model the signals that he or she expects. While espousing such thoughtful insights into her leadership orientation, Kala eagerly admitted that her leadership actions were incongruent with what she espoused. Her position was that she believed her heart was in the right place, but politically, her hands were tied. In response to this statement, I pushed Kala to expound on what she meant by her "hands were tied." Reluctantly she asked what was it that I wanted to know? I informed her that since we agreed to have a candid conversation, I would like her to unpack the incongruence between her theories and her actions. I told her that there was significant evidence that her leadership actions suggested that she was not thoroughly empathetic.

She appeared to lead from an orientation of selective empathy, and it appeared that her willingness to be empathetic to her direct reports who worked in certain zip codes and communities was high. Conversely, people living in other zip codes were discounted and did not receive equitable treatment. Kala shared that "do as I say and not as I do" can have some benefits. She stated that while she did not always align her actions to her words, it was her hope that her direct reports, all of whom were also leading teams of people, do as she said and not as she did.

She has pointed out that since that role, she is more cognizant of the necessity for, and the impact of, leading from an empathetic orientation. She also stated that her commitment to connect with every direct report in a personal and authentic way has helped her to not miss those who are often overlooked, thereby making everyone feel supported.

The Necessary Shift
Toward Radical Empathy

Kala's story shows that we should prioritize people over politics, even when it means defying the powers that be because this will inevitably speak to your legacy. Educators should consider what they want their leadership legacy to be and to make sure it always aligns their actions to their values; that is the measure of character and the true test of shifting towards radical empathy. Kala's focus was on the politics and procedures to activate sound leadership in her direct reports. She needed to pivot towards prioritizing equitable support for all of her teammates regardless of the type of school they served or zip codes where they were located. Making this decision would have married the First Seven and Second Seven Commitments. The radically empathetic leader is one who strikes a healthy balance between the two sets of commitments.

Another way to make the shift towards radically empathetic leadership is to look at the often spoken of dichotomy between "Maslow vs. Blooms." The radically empathetic practitioner prioritizes the basic needs of children or adults over the focus on their depth of knowledge, intellectual, or academic development. In aligning a radically empathetic approach to Maslow's hierarchy of needs, one must prioritize the basic needs of those with whom they come into contact, prior to the higher order needs such as educational accomplishments. Maslow's Hierarchy of Needs is a motivational theory in the field of psychology that comprises a five-tier model and depiction of human needs. This is usually represented as a hierarchical set of needs within a pyramid, with the needs that are lower down being of utmost importance before individuals can attend to the needs that are higher up on the pyramid. It is imperative that radically empathetic leaders prioritize people's basic needs like food, clean water, sleep, and clothing. While it might make the most professional sense to be concerned about educational accomplishments, the radically empathetic leader does not overlook the basics first. Bloom's Taxonomy is a classification system that many educators use to distinguish different levels of human cognition such as thinking, learning, and understanding.

Bloom's Taxonomy posits that there are three hierarchical models used to classify educational learning objectives into levels of complexity and specificity. For example, in the K-12 classroom, the three cover the learning objectives in cognitive, affective, and the sensory domains. As a framework, this has been applied by generations of grades K-12 teachers and university professors as a supplement to their pedagogical delivery to determine the level of rigor of a lesson. The six levels that this taxonomy uses are knowledge, comprehension, application, analysis, synthesis, and evaluation. While these levels are important to the intellectual and academic pursuits of students, the radically empathetic leader always prioritizes the tenets of Maslow's Hierarchy (basic human needs) over Bloom's Taxonomy (educational learning.)

Chapter 8.

The Real Color of the School-to-Prison Pipeline

The topic of the school to prison pipeline is of utmost importance to me both personally and professionally. When I wrote the book, *Prisoners of Presidents* I introduced, in detail, the connection between radical empathy and dismantling the educational genocide taking place in U.S. schools. Consequently, it is imperative that I share in great detail the connection between radical empathy and dismantling the school-to-prison-pipeline. As such you will notice that this essay is unpacked with a keener level of detail than the other essays. This is because although you could read *Prisoners or Presidents*, I could not in good conscience write a book about radical empathy in schools without addressing the topic here as well.

Whenever the question of what the genesis of the school-to-prison-pipeline is comes up for discussion, many who are conversant with this phenomenon will espouse that it starts in the classroom with disciplinary action against students (OSS). Others will purport that it has its foundation in a place that is much more sinister, policy at the school district and state legislature levels. In 2017, one example that gained national attention occurred in the midwestern region of the United States. The Missouri Statute which took effect on January 1, 2017 could give students criminal records by charging them with a class E felony for fighting in school. For example, the new law states that regardless of age and grade level of a student, if they are involved in a fight on a school bus or in school, and this is witnessed by a School Resource Officer (SRO), they should be arrested and charged with a class E felony. Educational policy controversy is not limited to any region in the United States. However, I want to highlight the Midwest because this is where one of the more egregious manifestations of a controversial policy feeding the school-to-prison-pipeline (STPP) occurred.

We live in an educational world that constantly examines and dissects data from a trend-analysis and comparative data standpoint. I often reflect on one of the brilliant intellectual nuggets of my leadership north star, Nelson Mandela. I wonder, compared to other developed countries; how have we treated our children lately?

President Mandela pointed out that there can be no keener revelation of a community or society's soul than the way in which it treats its children. One revelation that is clear about contemporary U.S. society with regards to the treatment of our children is steeped in contradiction to this belief. In 2016 given the recent legislation that threatens to charge students with a felony if they are involved in a fight that results in "infliction of emotional distress."

Historical Context

The Juvenile Justice and Delinquency Prevention Act of 1974 (P.L. 93-415, 88 Stat. 1109) was the first major federal legislation to shape the content of state policy on the juvenile justice system. It was enacted in response to sustained criticism of the juvenile court system that reached its peak in three Supreme Court decisions in the late 1960s and early 1970s. Through this act Congress created federal standards for the treatment of juvenile offenders and provided financial incentives for state systems to comply with those standards. The act had two main goals:

- to remove juveniles from adult jails and prisons, and

- to end the practice of using the juvenile court system as a means of sending both criminal and noncriminal minors to prison like institutions for rehabilitation.

The theory of rehabilitation holds that people's behavior, especially young people's behavior, can be changed so that individuals can re- enter and function normally in society. Enlightening and empowering youth to become normally functioning adults in society is a hallmark of schools and school districts, and one would hope that it's the same desire of the legislative and judicial branch, but this is probably wishful thinking. Case in point, the recent deaths of several unarmed Black men, especially our young boys, compounded by the continued spike in and disparity in out-of-school-suspensions of Black and LatinX children has cast a glaring light on a deeply entrenched problem, one that criminalizing non-criminal behaviors will not address. It is no wonder that Black children, especially boys, experience and view the criminal justice system and law enforcement and society-at-large differently than their non-Black counterparts.

A Contemporary Reality

During the week of December 12, 2016 there were announcements and public sharing of two monumental occurrences in the show-me state of Missouri. Both of these announcements could potentially forever change one community's response to how we treat our children. In 2021, there is still some confusion about the new law, and this was compounded by the fact that educators of several districts and news media outlets have acted as Monday morning quarterbacks about the changes in an existing statue. Apparently the most notable change states that if students are involved in a fight and there is evidence that the victim suffered from "infliction of emotional distress," the aggressor may be charged with a class three felony. In one instance, a spokesperson for a St. Louis, Missouri school district pointed out that essentially, "this well-publicized fear is that the new statutes could mean that a scuffle at the bus stop, or a hyperactive youth harasses another by pulling on their hair, could imbue children with the stain of serious criminal charges from which they can never make themselves clean." Under the law, harassment is defined as any act that causes emotional distress. This law essentially elevates harassment from a school discipline issue or, at worse, heightens a misdemeanor to a felony.

Reflective Questions

Allow me to pose several questions that may have crossed your mind as well. When our founding policymakers conceptualized the three branches of government, is this what they envisioned and imagined for our children? Did they imagine that at least two of the three branches (judicial and legislative) would make decisions that give one the impression that they effectively collaborate to discriminate against the least amongst us; our children? Did they imagine that those individuals who were entrusted with the power to govern and legislate would do so in an arbitrary and capricious manner in some instances? Is the new Missouri law another attempt to perpetuate this disenfranchisement of some people or groups and offer very little protection, hope, and possibilities to those who are the most underserved and underestimated? This law, if it lives up to the hype of impacting the trajectory of our children negatively, will certainly nourish the school-to-prison-pipeline. There should be no wonder about whether there is plenty of evidence to substantiate the claims that many in positions of power are actively feeding this phenomenon.

In 2008, former Judge of the Pennsylvania Luzerne County Court Mark Arthur Ciavarella with fellow judge Michael Conahan, in the "Kids for Cash" scandal was sentenced to 28 years in prison. These judges were receiving payments (up to 1 million dollars) for every child that they sent to the juvenile detention center. This case is a textbook manifestation of the failure of the judicial system to protect our children and feed the mass incarceration machine.

Shirking Responsibility

The architects of the new Missouri law seems to punt the responsibility of addressing student misbehavior to school and school district leaders, not to mention it's an apparent criminalization of behaviors that can probably benefit from an approach that is focused on a socio-psychological or socio- emotional approach. My conversations with the stakeholders who this will potentially impact the most reveals that school leaders are worried about the impact on their daily response and practices around guiding students. Additionally, many secondary schools students are worried and concerned about the implications for them. The rhetoric surrounding the new policy as echoed by the stakeholders whom it will most affect (students and school personnel) is one that needs to be addressed and tamed through a common sense and empathetic approach. I have considered a few questions as we look at the STPP.

- Within the school context, will we see some teachers and school leaders now threatening students with calling the police instead of calling a parent?

- One highly effective Missouri high school principal shared three perspectives of students which sums up their concerns during a cafeteria dialogue they stated/asked; "We should not get involved in physical altercations anyway." "Is the system trying to get rid of us?" "Will you as our principal send us through the criminal justice system if we fight?"

· Are we saying that students have this propensity to engage in pugilistic encounters? If they do, what are the root causes of such deviant behaviors? Should our focus be on punishment or redirection?

· Is this a contemporary version of the Voting Rights Act (1965)? There is no longer a need for a literacy test to disenfranchise a large but potentially powerful group of people. A felony prevents one from being enfranchised, and this certainly seems like a strategic and targeted way to do so.

It's tricky and concerning that both laws (permit less conceal and carry constituency; and the criminalization of an in school physical or other altercation that results in "emotional distress.") were enacted within days of each other. A question to ponder is; How about the perception that a definition or characterization of the same incident of physical assault, bullying, harassing, or fighting that results in the "infliction of emotional distress" will take on a different meaning based on the community in which it occurred? Essentially, incidents that are deemed to be law-violating in schools in predominantly Black and LatinX communities these same incidents are perceived to be minor infractions or disagreements in white schools.

We have seen many instances where the same behaviors committed by Black and white students are given a different characterization. An altercation between two Black students is often a fight; conversely, a similar interaction between two non-Black students is often coined a "misunderstanding." This sharing is not from a race-baiting or biased stance, but instead is based on enough empirical evidence from several credible practitioners including my own first-hand accounts.

The school-to-prison-pipeline data is daunting and some policy makers appear to send a pellucidly clear message about their thoughts regarding our youth; especially Black and LatinX youth. Although they make up only 18% of students enrolled in public schools, Black students account for 42% of the out of school suspensions daily. Can you imagine the disparity in the numbers of the aforementioned students who will be sent to juvenile justice detention centers for offenses that were historically addressed by school personnel? Although my faith in the American Civil Liberties Union (ACLU) in its continued fight for the voiceless is at an all-time high, I wonder if some loophole in this and similar thinking and/or legislature will somehow victimize and criminalize our children and balloon the recidivism rates of juvenile justice centers and alternative schools.

Prediction

As a result of this new legislature in the state of Missouri, the increase in Out of School Suspensions (OSS) may not double, but there is the potential for the drop-out rate to slide deeper into the red. If a student gets involved in a fight, regardless if they were the aggressor or not, instead of facing a possible felony charge, there is the possibility that they may choose to evade the legal system by skipping and eventually never returning to school. After all, contrary to the belief of some adults in the arena of education, juvenile justice centers (Juvie) and some alternative schools are no "walk-in-the-park."

There is universal understanding and agreement that the adolescent years are the most rebellious years, and if our adults in the arenas of education and social service are not prepared to adequately address the tide of behaviors from a socio-emotional stance, we will certainly contribute to the mass incarceration of Black and LatinX people, especially adolescent males.

Conspiracy theorists, sociologists, and even some criminal justice pundits have pointed out that there are those in positions of power who are committed to relegating Black and LatinX students into a place of challenge, and through laws and policy such as the aforementioned, there is the inevitability of a ballooning Pipeline and mass incarceration.

Opting In or Opting Out

Regardless of the veracity of the new Missouri law, as teachers, school, and district leaders, we can choose to combat or contribute to the mass incarceration of our youth. The power rests in which side of this dichotomous coin we choose, contributor or combatants?

Contributors

- School and district personnel who suspend students for minor infractions of the school's student code of conduct.

- School and district personnel who indict students based on the mistakes and records from previous years, previous schools, or academic deficits that give the appearance of "hopelessness."

- School and district personnel who are less likely to lead and teach with empathy and compassion.

- School and district personnel who are more concerned with meeting testing targets than empowering and enlightening youth under their tutelage.

- School and district personnel who are partially committed to providing students with multiple opportunities to succeed.

- School and district personnel who through their actions demonstrate that non-White youth have a genetic predisposition for violence, failure, and mediocrity.

- School and district personnel who will unhesitatingly support policy even when it contradicts their moral and philosophical stance.

Combatants

- School and district personnel who humanize their data by acknowledging and recognizing that at the end of every data point, there is a person.

- School and district personnel who blend their sound pedagogy with an empathetic and compassionate approach.

- School and district personnel understand the dynamic between policy and practice and have the leadership sophistication to successfully navigate them.

- School and district personnel who look at our youth and encourage their potential while envisioning their endless possibilities for an enhanced life.

- School and district personnel who are willing to provide multiple opportunities to students that enable their success.

- School and district personnel who demonstrate a commitment to invest in and not arrest our youth.

- School and district personnel who understand and embody that a critical part of our very make-up and existence is to shield children from the other societal institutions such as the courts and penal system. As educators, we commit to and should not waver from this commitment to educate our children in a safe, secure, and opportunistic environment.

- School and district personnel who understand that we have to entrust school leaders and the trained and qualified related service providers (i.e., psychologist, counselor) to empower children to successfully deal with stressful situations? We have agreed that schools are a microcosm of the larger society. Since most of our interactions in society are characterized by a dynamic that involves varying levels of stress, it is incumbent upon the institutions where children spend most of their adolescent years (schools) to equip them for the future.

Dawn's Story

It was approximately 07:30 AM and my team of deans and I were outside on our morning post welcoming students to school, fixing their uniforms, adjusting their neck ties, and asking about their readiness for school that day. This was our typical morning routine at this amazing high school in the southeast quadrant of Washington, DC. We enjoyed it for several reasons, including the relationships that it allowed us to develop with our students and their parents, many of whom dropped their children off to school. On this particular day, the call came over the radio with a code that said that there was an assault of an adult. Upon hearing of the classroom location, I remembered sprinting into the building, up the three flights of stairs to Ms. T's classroom. Ms. T was one of our dynamic English language arts teachers. She was teaching her first period class when Dawn, a student in the 12th grade had her head on the desk and appeared to be sleeping. Ms. T using the pedagogical strategy of proximity placed her hand on Dawn's shoulder and asked her to sit up, to which she sat up for 10 seconds and resumed her sleeping posture. About 5 minutes after, Ms. T approached her again, tapped her on the shoulder and asked if she needed to go and wash her face to stay awake, to which Dawn replied, "Leave me alone." placing her head on the desk again and closing her eyes. After 30 minutes, Ms. T. circled back to Dawn's desk, tapped her on the shoulder, at which point Dawn got up from the desk, pushed Ms. T and blurted out, "Leave me the f*ck alone." Ms. T, tripped on a desk and fell to the floor, at which point the school security, police, and administrators were called to the classroom. When I arrived at the classroom, Dawn was crying hysterically and being held by the school police. I was surprised that of all of the students, it was Dawn who was involved in this incident.

Dawn was an honor roll student who had not had one disciplinary infraction in her four years at the school. I walked Dawn to my office during which time she was still hysterical, crying and uttering that Ms. T should not have touched her or prevented her from sleeping. I reminded Dawn of her obligation to abide by the rules of the classroom and school. She said she understood but was really tired. I inquired some more about why she put her hands on the teacher because that singular action could likely get her suspended and possibly expelled. By the time we got to my office, Dawn was still crying uncontrollably and shared with me that while Ms. T was at home sleeping last night, she (Dawn) was "sucking &#%!" so that her mother could get money to buy cocaine. At this very moment my heart had a sinking feeling and I summoned the social worker, counselor, and nurse to my office. Our investigation found that Dawn was one of two girls living at home with their mother. She was regularly subjected to performing sexual acts with multiple men for money most of which her mother used for food, but in other instances, used the money to feed an addiction to narcotics. When Dawn was asked why she did not report this to anyone else or consider leaving the home, she stated that she believed that if she had left, her mother would then impose the same expectation on her 10-year-old sister.

The school and district's policy in every instance of a student assaulting a teacher is expulsion from the school. I made an exception this time. I made the decision not to expel or even suspend Dawn. In my judgement, Dawn's and her family's current reality did not warrant punishment, but support. My decision not to impose any discipline on Dawn resulted in approximately 50% of my staff writing me letters of disapproval and many of them wouldn't even speak to me for two weeks following the incident. As always, most secrets or information that should remain in confidence are often leaked. Unfortunately, in this case, the information about Dawn's home life was leaked. Once teachers had a fuller picture, I received apologies from many of them who were initially critical of my decision. Several of them offered acknowledgements that they believed I made the right decision. They also reinforced their commitments to teach, lead, and support Dawn and all of our students from a radically empathetic approach. According to one teacher, "you never know what our students are surviving."

The Department of Social Services was summoned, they investigated and provided Dawn's mother with the family support and rehabilitation needed. Dawn was able to accept a full academic scholarship to a university in Pennsylvania, where she took on guardianship of her sister, and subsequently graduated with a Bachelor of Science and Master of Science in Social Work. Had I decided to expel Dawn, that would have been a decision devoid of radical empathy. The decision would have likely resulted in a possible criminal record for assault and hers would be yet another name of a student added to the school-to-prison-pipeline roster.

The Necessary Shift
Toward Radical Empathy

I cannot even conceive of the shift in school leader training that will become necessary beginning January 1, 2017. Instead of a focus on critical pedagogy and the key performance indicators that measures outputs and outcomes, school districts throughout Missouri and nationally will need to prepare their principals and assistant principals to decipher how to criminalize or not criminalize a student's violation of the code of conduct. Regardless of the laws and policies that are out in place to inadvertently fuel the school-to-prison-pipeline the primary combatants are superintendents and principals.

As a district leader, I often visited alternative sites or juvenile detention facilities. The staff and leaders in those situations are doing amazing work. The youth who I encounter are filled with potential and promise, but are weighed down by despair and pain. As educational leaders, teachers, and policy makers, we cannot afford to allow empathy to evade us. If empathy evades us, effective leadership will elude us. This law and similar policies will undoubtedly cause our children to suffer. Remember, if we genuinely believe that we can tell a lot about a society or community by the way it treats its constituents and the least amongst us, we must act accordingly.

Natasha's Story

While there are dedicated and committed district and school leaders whose daily actions result in positive outcomes for thousands of students, there are those occurrences that serve as reminders about the necessity for radical empathy training. The training that is not often found in the professional development plan. Natasha and I were on our third lap of the track during our walk. This setting from our conversation was her idea because in her words, "I spend so much time in the building that on average I only experience about 30 minutes of sunlight during the winter." Natasha was in her third year as the principal of the middle school. Here, she and her team were expected to produce improvements in student achievement and simultaneously retain one hundred percent of their teachers. The instability at the school was problematic as they were about to get their 4th principal in 7 years.

I was selected to serve as Natasha's successor and reached out to her for a meeting. She agreed and chose to meet for 30 minutes at a nearby track if I was willing to walk with her. I had several questions for her about her journey as a school leader. I was interested in information about her time at the current school. I also wanted to know what advice or guidance she would give to me as I prepare to take over a school from a seasoned leader. During the first two laps, Natasha talked about how her journey as an educator started. She was one of three children who grew up in the suburbs of Baltimore, Maryland. She and her two siblings lived with their mother and father who were both college professors, and constantly sermonized about the importance of education. She laughed out loud when she asked me if I could imagine living with two college professors, and whether I could imagine what the dinner conversations were like? We both smiled and she continued sharing about her own experiences in grades K-12, most of which were spent in private schools that were expensive. She shared that for her last two years of high school, she was enrolled in a public school. According to her, she believes that her parents made this decision as a punishment and to teach her a lesson, since she started to increase her social time with friends who they believed were not as academically inclined as she was. Natasha stopped, looked at me and in a moment of reflection told me that she believed that the blessing from her parents' punishment allowed her to see the incredible brilliance and talent that walked the halls and sat in classes of the city's public schools. She shared that she attributes her experience during her last two years in high school as the inspiration to become a public-school teacher.

As we started our final lap around the track and continued our conversation, we had been together for almost one hour, when I posed the question of what she would have done differently, and what is one piece of advice that she would give to me. Over the years, having transitioned between many leadership roles and succeeding a diverse group of leaders, I have found that these two questions remain constant in their importance. Without skipping a beat in her long, athletic walking stride, Natasha responded that her commitment to the school district's assessment and student discipline policies have always been a struggle for her as she attempted to balance doing what's right by students with compliance to policies that were not in the student's best interest, but that of policy makers. She shared that in her three years at the school, she had suspended approximately 320 students each year, and had recommended at least 60 of them for expulsion from the district. I asked her if there were alternatives to suspension that she could have selected, and whether she believed that I would be faced with the same challenge. She stopped, looked at me and shared that there are two pieces of advice she wanted to give. The first was for me to understand that she had seen the devastating impact that her suspension and expulsion numbers have had on students; students who were disproportionately Black and LatinX. She talked about the fact that she and her team had suspended homeless students and students with special needs who in many instances, never came back to school after their second and third suspensions. Natasha then told me that being a principal is like being a pastor. In espousing this analogy, she said that your students and their families are your flock, and you have to be good at protecting them. "I did not do that well." As we made our way off of the track and back to her office, she paused at a bench just outside the gates of the track, offered that we sit and answered my final question about what advice she would give to me. "I don't think this is advice, but in the past three years, I have spent six days a week in this school, including many Saturdays." "I arrived in the building before the sun came up, and never left until it disappeared in the sky;

and to think that at the end of the day I my actions have caused dozens of students to drop out of school with uncertain futures, and now I am out of a job." "I would never have suspended those students if I knew what the impact of my decisions would be so far-reaching and life-changing. I never took the time to find out about their lives outside of school." She stood up, extended her hands to shake mine, and wished me well.

I left the time and conversation thinking about what I wanted to do differently. I wondered if Natasha, at age 41 had other social or family commitments that could have inspired her to leave the building early some days. I even felt judgmental as I thought about how dare her to suspend that many students, and how her actions must have clearly funneled them into the school-to-prison-pipeline. On the way to my car, I vowed never to make the same mistakes that she made as a principal.

Two weeks after our conversation at the track, I received a meeting invitation on a Friday morning to meet with the superintendent that afternoon. Although we had a meeting on our schedules, it was not slated to occur for another month. It was at that meeting where I received the news that earlier that morning, Natasha's family found her dead in her bedroom. She had gone to sleep the night before and never woke up. To this day, our conversation, her vulnerability, guidance, and advice still rings in my ear. I still wonder what amazing things she could have done given her experiences as a principal and how introspective and reflective she had become after those three years as a school leader.

Chapter 9.

Is it Time to Change Your Professional Diet?

The truth is, I do not have the gift of a singing voice, but I grew up listening to Bob Marley, The Mighty Sparrow, Fela Kuti, Notorious B.I.G, The Fugees, Frank Sinatra, and Tupac. Sonically, that was the extent of my musical diet and I recognized at an early enough age that it was very limiting, and it would behoove me to expand it. It was not until I decided to embrace artists such as Kenny G, Otis Redding, Al Green, Chuck Jackson, Luciano Pavarotti, Placido Domingo, Louis Armstrong, Faith Hill, Celine Dion, Keith Urban, Whitney Houston, and Patti Label, that I was able to ingest more variety into my musical diet, thereby expanding it in a great way.

Based on its medical definition, a diet consists of the things that we regularly consume to improve and positively impact our wellbeing. Our diet is what we ingest, and most likely will determine our ability to perform, and may even impact the quality of our outputs and existence in every aspect of our lives. By its very definition, the practice of dieting is the food and drink we regularly consumed for nourishment, and/or a very specific reason; especially to lose weight and improve your quality of life. Dieting to lose weight, especially excess weight, is for the primary purposes of increasing mobility, improving the functionality of one's heart, getting traction with every pursuit, and leading a healthier life.

This juxtaposition of one's professional diet with a medical diet is not in any way intended to be pejorative or purposefully demeaning; but it is intended to stimulate your thinking and inspire a moment of reflection.

My questions to you are how has your professional diet been lately? Are you embracing the right professional diet? I want you to think about eight questions to gauge if your professional diet is what it should be. The reason for the number eight is simply because numerologists tell us that eight is the number of new beginnings. If you realize that your professional diet is not what it should be at this time, all isn't lost; here is an opportunity for a new beginning. Unlike a medical diet, your professional diet should not be limited to what you ingest, but it should definitely be shaped by your intended outputs for your professional journey and how the intended change in diet will impact others.

1. **Are you carrying around professional weight or baggage that prevents you from maximizing your performance?** Examples of professional baggage includes – a defeatist mentality and attitude; being constantly critical of peers

and direct reports; being guided by your unconscious bias or blind spots, unwillingness to share effective practices; exhibiting discriminatory and prejudicial tendencies in a pluralistic environment; unwillingness to be empathetic, focus on evaluation instead of coaching, unwillingness to collaborate.

2. **What does your professional diet consist of? Have you had the same professional diet for the past five, ten, fifteen years?** Example; unwillingness to read up-to-date books/ articles that are aligned to your professional practice (read one in the past 30 days); examining and utilizing leadership practices from outside of the education or current profes-sional arena; intentionality to maintain a work-life-balance (professional and personal self-care); based on the feedback from peers and colleagues, you lead, speak, or espouse the same practices in the same way that you did three, four, or five years ago.

3. **Have you maintained the same professional circle or have you expanded to persons outside of this district, your childhood friend or college friends, or your graduate class?** Example: surrounding yourself with individuals

who are positive and solutions oriented, embody humility, understand that data is important but at the end of every data point is a person (humanity outweighs data); surround yourself with people who do not always agree with you (YES people).

4. **Have you sought after professional development (PD) outside of the organization or district's offering?** Example: not just a PD out of the district or organization, but an opportunity that is value-added which does not exist locally. Exploring targeted and differentiated professional development that benefits you and elevates the performance of the team.

5. **Have you facilitated a professional development or provided thought leadership/partnership to peers or other leaders within the past 6 months?** Example: you have a willingness to share practices, strategies, and plans that have worked well for you and your team. Have you recommended an article or book that aligns to the team or organization's mission?

6. **How do you know that your claimed expertise in any given field is robust or authentic?** Example: you are not

braggadocio about your ability; especially if you do not have a track record or data/evidence to support your claim. Has your contribution to the team or organization added value that is measurable?

7. **Are you setting and keeping the bar high for yourself and others?** Example: the bar includes leading from a place of empathy and compassion; being mission and vision driven; continuously anchoring your daily actions in exemplary practices; engaging positively with ALL stakeholders.

8. **Have you selected a mentor who can provide the "right" and prudent professional guidance to you?** Example: You are consuming cutting edge and up to date information, research, and other resources in your given field of work; your mentor is an expert, has a proven track record of excellence, is brutally honest, and is available to you with consistency.

Medical Doctors and nutritionists advise that we change our diet as we age to increase our longevity and ensure a healthy lifestyle. In many instances, we are fully aware that a refusal to adhere to the doctor's advice to change our diet, stop smoking, or exercise more frequently can have detrimental and, in some instances, fatal consequences. Yet, many of us are not willing to activate the needed change because we are comfortable with our current practices; we are afraid to be vulnerable; or by our own evaluation, we just do not believe that our current practices are unhealthy or mediocre at best. There is a plethora of data that echoes the fact that the unwillingness to change or make the needed and suggested adjustments to a medical diet can significantly reduce one's longevity and may even result in fatality. Similarly, an unwillingness to make the necessary adjustments to one's professional diet along the professional journey of choice or calling may have the same results.

Making the right changes to your professional diet should not be limited to the bare minimum as outlined in the aforementioned 8 questions. Similar to a medical diet, changing your professional diet requires intentionality, personal sacrifice, and commitment. Such sacrifice and commitment require a shift in your beliefs, values, and practices. Anyone can read the latest text or leadership book and article, which allows them to regurgitate the typical pleasant sounding educational rhetoric in their professional circles. That does not equate to effectiveness as a leader and inspirer of people.

Having the right professional diet allows one to be a motivator of one's peers and direct reports, so that they may be inspired to go above and beyond the call of duty. Whether you are in the role of a teacher, associate, leader, policy maker, or proletariat, I encourage each of you to make the necessary adjustments to your professional diet and remember that if the leaders are not professionally healthy, the team or organization will need intensive care. Some of the most successful teachers and school leaders who model what it means to have a healthy professional diet are those who have committed to their professional development, maintaining a balance of work and family and social life by leaving their offices at a reasonable time, and building on a commitment to a sanctuary of church or exercise. For these individuals who are experiencing this success, a tremendous value add to their professional diet is when they volunteer to coach their peers on the strategies that have led to their success.

Ruth's Story

Ruth had achieved many accolades in her 12 years as an educator. She was named Teacher of the Year. She had served as an educator in a 90/90/90 school and was achieving great professional success. Yet, as Ruth sat across from me in a pensive posture and deep moment of reflection, she attributed the end of her 15-year marriage to her inability to maintain work-life-balance. She had a "poor professional diet" and it was creating challenges for her in other areas of her life.

Ruth was an African American woman, stood 5 feet 9 inches tall, and at age 45, could easily be thought of as being in her early thirties. While Ruth's success was considered a model for the district and for leaders nationally, her personal life was suffering. Her two children, one in middle and the other in high school, were not receiving the benefits of the care and dedication that she gave to other people's children daily. In what appeared to be a pensive stance, she leaned back in her leather chair behind her desk, looked out the window and said to me; "You know, before the principalship, I felt like a model parent and supportive spouse. Next to God, my family was the most important thing to me, then it started to feel as if I was now married to the job. I wanted to be the first person in the building each day, and the never-ending list of to do's inspired me to be the last person to leave the building."

She said that in hindsight, she believed that I owed her children as well as my ex-husband an apology. Had she known at the beginning of her principalship what she knew sitting across the desk from me, she would have had a quite different life. Turning to me, she was quick to assert that while she was happy and enjoying work, she sometimes wished that she could turn back the hands of time. Ruth pointed out that she saw many signs that her professional diet was poor. Her neglect of her children where they only saw and spent quality time with her at weekends, and the fact that she started scheduling intimacy with her husband. Her diet should have included professional self-care, quality time with her family, and participation in more targeted professional development. She asserted with a smile; I am finally focusing on my diet every way.

"The weight I gained this year is because I only have time to eat in the evenings after my breakfast (which is usually a coffee), has resulted in 10 more pounds, well more like 15 but who is counting?" Then as she laughed out loud she said, "I am more focused on my professional diet as well. I attend at least one conference a month, read two articles monthly, and one book each month. I must get better in my last few years."

Then she paused for two minutes and asked, "Do you know that more than 90 percent of principals die within the first decade after retiring from this work?" Before I could respond, she fired off two other questions that were more rhetorical in nature. I wonder how many years I will live after my retirement in ten years. How many principals do you believe are aware of this statistic? Ruth leaned over and said with a crack in her voice, "I just want to be able to retire, and have more than ten years to enjoy it. One day I will apologize to my family; even my ex-husband," as she chuckled.

The Necessary Shift Toward Radical Empathy

The radically empathetic leader who is intentional about the necessary shift in their professional diet should take a page out of Ruth's book and focus on their professional diet. That diet should include professional self-care, quality time with family, and participation in more targeted professional development. This shift should include membership in groups that are healthy socially, and professional organizations that add tremendous value to one's career trajectory. Like Ruth, this shift around one's professional diet should include reading articles and books in and outside of your chosen field of work. The radically empathetic leader's professional diet should include a focus on personal, spiritual, and professional health. What is your spiritual or religious belief? If you believe it is important, make some time for your spiritual/religious growth and development as well. Make time to take care of your nutritional intake. You only have one body, take care of it. It is critical for you to build up your physical and emotional stamina and staying power. Although this is not an exhaustive list of suggested actions to make the shift towards a healthy professional diet, remember a journey of 1,000 miles begins with a single step. Take that step and outlive the ten-year prediction for longevity after retirement.

Chapter 10.

The Unsexy Nature of Data Driven Schools

Data? What data? Which data? Why data? Data days? Data meetings? Data protocols? Data driven? Data dense? Data rich?

Are you aware that data, any data in the school, district, on the team, or within the organization's context loses its validity when it is apparent that we fail to realize that **real children or adults are attached to each data point?** As school leaders grapple with the aforementioned questions and ponder on the most effective ways to anchor their work in a data driven culture, they are often forced to decide on the key performance indicators (KPIs) or objectives and key results (OKRs) that are best suited for every situation. They are also on a tightrope trying to ascertain which ones will drive the right outcomes.

The most perilous issue for leaders is the disconnect between rich sets of data points and the actual people behind those numbers. Questions often asked in data driven schools are, "What performance indicators are best to drive towards performance, and in which school leaders should truly anchor their strategic plans?" As you read this essay, you may wonder why I have chosen to write in such a satirical expository and confusing manner, which does not necessarily meet the ELA standard of Common Core or College and Career Readiness.

You may even predict that I will likely end up on the wrong side of the rubric in a highly rigorous academic assignment of an English language arts class. The answer is simple; this is the exact state of intellectual frustration and mental confusion that teachers and school leaders feel when forced to create "data driven cultures" that are disconnected from the reality of the work. They are the mandates of data walls, weekly surface level data meetings, data reviews that are often not shared with the pertinent stakeholder, who the data affects the most, and data charts, tables, and diagrams that are abstract, and barely stimulate investment from those who are tasked with examining them. Data driven school and district cultures do not succeed when we fail to recognize and highlight the fact that **there are children attached to each data point.**

As school district leaders or policy makers, do we ever wonder if current practices around creating data driven cultures are the most prudent way for us to encourage our astute, dedicated, and committed teachers and school leaders to spend their time? How or on what should they really spend their time, given the competing priorities that educators, particularly principals are faced with? Here is one suggestion; select 3 to 5 major undertakings or priorities for the year, and "ride them until the wheels fall off." Policy makers, district, and school leaders, may I suggest that it is impractical and not prudent to have a new data point or priority each week, and ascribe the failures to achieve scalable outcomes to the principal, practitioner, or implementer's inability to effectively utilize data?

Food for Thought

13, 520, 120... During the early part of the school year, and at various other times (monthly), these numbers were shared with a group of middle and high school principals. Yes, I recognize and understand that principals and school leadership teams have competing priorities as they navigate the daily execution of their responsibility to lead one of our nation's most important institutions, however the numbers above are one of the 3 to 5 priorities and data points that I have and will always strongly encourage school principals and district leaders to focus on. **13** is the number of weeks that we have been in school this year; **520** is the number of hours a principal would have worked during those **13** weeks if they worked 40-hour weeks (try 70-hour weeks); and **120** is the average number of hours the identified group of principals spent on the deliverable of observing and supporting instruction and pedagogical improvements in their schools. These numbers, although NOT acceptable (less than ¼ of time spent on instruction and teacher support), were not shared as an indictment on their leadership ability, but as a data point to stimulate their reflective practitioner muscles and activate change. The truth is the principals in the surveyed group are amongst the most talented and dedicated anywhere in these United States. My intent and goal, as is the goal of data dives or data meetings should never be to denigrate, but to inspire immediate strategic action.

The Myth of Data Driven Cultures

At the basic level of creating a data driven culture, data walls are necessary in the classrooms and throughout the buildings. Yes, this is a tremendous addition to the academic aesthetics of the school environment but as a stand-alone resource it does little to enhance practice. I repeatedly encourage school leaders and their teams to make a concerted effort to know every student by name, family connections, current home circumstance, their desires, and post-secondary plans. I ask them repeatedly, how the adults may help them achieve their goals. Believe it or NOT, every student who walks through the doors of our schools each day has goals. Consider this fact; professional sport teams (NBA, NFL, NHL, boxing, and MMA) utilize data when scouting opponents. The data points that they examine are never numbers and charts that are devoid of actual names, photos, and even videos of the actual persons/athletes and their plays. Creating targets that appear to be tangible, real, and are known, allows the human element to guide critical decisions, and increases the likelihood of favorable outcomes. The state mandated assessments and achievement outcomes for districts are easily attainable when every adult sees the data points and the connections to students.

Interact with the Data

During my tenure as a principal in Baltimore City and Washington, DC, one non-traditional way that I embarked upon to encourage people to interact with the data was the home visits that every teachers and staff member was strongly encouraged to participate in prior to the start of the school year, and several times during the year. During a game that we named "The Amazing Race," we divided the 126 teachers and staff into teams, and we visited the homes of each enrolled student during an exhausting but fun 4-6 hours. The team that returned to the school first having contacted each student on their list won a significant prize (dinner with yours truly). I believed that teachers and staff needed to see, feel, and make authentic connections to that community, instead of allowing what they read or heard about the students, families, and over-all state of the residents to guide their data driven decisions when serving the community. We did this for each year I was the principal. After each of the community visits, there were many authentic and emotional reactions from teachers and leaders who made those visits. Some of the quotes from them included "I could not have imagined that parents had so much confidence in our ability to teach their children." "As bright as Samantha is, I did not realize that she and her siblings had to share a single bed or sleep on the floor." "The respect that parents and community members have for teachers and staff at this school is unbelievable. I would not have known had I not come into the community." Many teachers, and in some instances the accompanying news and media persons have said, "I believe that every teacher and principal in this country should start their school year with such visits."

The impact that such school visits into the communities had on the culture of schools are both measurable and immea-surable. The authentic relationships that teachers, staff, and students formed resulted in increased investment by students in the business of school, schooling, and more specifically, their desire to do well on all assessments and tests for both themselves and their teachers. Additionally, those visits resulted in life-long connections and friendships between teachers, students, and community members.

As you lead to inspire change through data, consider the human being at the other end of the number, and it will likely increase your investment and that of your team in a data driven culture. For educators, it will behoove you to remember that at the end of every data point, there is a child; and in other instances, there are peers.

Andre's Story

A few years ago, Andre was the center of attention at his graduation party. His grandmother, aunts and uncles all bragged about how proud they were of him. He was the first person in the family to graduate at the top of his class. He was number 1 out of 230 students and had therefore earned honor of being the valedictorian of one of the school district's best high schools.

Two months later, after delivering his valedictory speech and celebrating, Andre experienced what he recalled and later described as a "shock and rude awakening." His college counselor at the local community college informed him that she enrolled him in 6 classes for his freshman year, but he would only receive credit for 2; as the other four were remedial courses. Based on the school and districts data, 230 students graduated in the class, and the highest academic achiever of the class (Andre) was not adequately prepared for college. Several district officials with whom I spoke sermonized that Andre is a "success story." He was "positively placed" after graduating high school and this was great for the district's data set. Was there any consideration for the fact that it may take Andre two additional years than his college cohort members in the affluent district to graduate? Data points/sets such as this which highlights the disproportionality and disadvantages of historically marginalized youth lose their value when a person/student is not attached to it. One practical and simplistic approach that I often encourage teachers and leaders to engage in is to use the photographs of students and other persons and attach it to every data point, and every data wall. Data walls should not be number, chart and diagram based. Practitioners should find ways to add photos or humanize the data!

The Necessary Shift
Toward Radical Empathy

Every school throughout the United States you visit will have some form or semblance of a data wall, data chart, or data room. Approximately 20 years ago, data-driven instruction and decision became the new shift, the paradigm that would change the way we conducted business in the K-12 education arena. According to education pundits and policy makers, it was one of those decision points that would stimulate the United States return to that place of education and technological preeminence it once held amongst the G8 and developed countries of the world.

If students in a school or district who are considered strong academically are required to take remedial courses during the initial years in college, this is a data point that must be embraced, analyzed, dissected, and solved before it becomes normalized. It is incredulous to sit around and celebrate and applaud students for excellence who will essentially be ill-prepared to compete in contemporary society in their post-secondary pursuits. Unfortunately, this practice only occurs and is acceptable in schools and districts that serve minority, under-privileged, and underserved children. If schools and their teams pivot towards treating students as individuals who they are invested in preparing for post-secondary success, instead of interacting with them purely based on the data point to satisfy a district's outcome, we will essentially perpetuate mediocrity around creating authentic data driven cultures for the students who need it the most.

Chapter 11.

Seven Steps to Radically Empathetic School Leadership

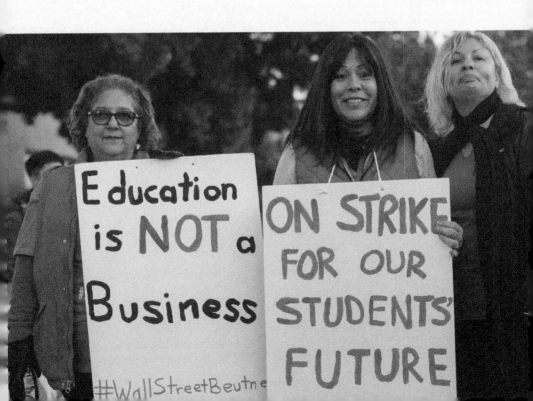

There is incredible power in the number seven. In ancient cultures, Hebrew included, there are many stories and instances where the number 7 has been used in profound ways in the Bible and other religious writings. The Seven Second-Chance™ philosophy is grounded in religious references, too. However, it is also based on experiences whereby student achievement and school turnaround occurred because of a willingness to furnish every student and teacher with multiple opportunities (14 opportunities) to be successful. Although not an exhaustive list, below are seven guidance points that school leaders can tap into as they continue, or pivot towards an empathetic and compassionate leadership orientation:

1. **Epitomize selfless leadership:** Leaders who build strong teams where every team member has high levels of investment are those who continuously demonstrate a genuine interest in people. Every week I send out a team/organization communication in which I strongly encourage every person to introduce themselves to someone, especially a student whose name they do not know, or with whom they do not interact. Find out what the student's plans are; where they reside; with whom do they live? Additionally, genuinely compliment colleagues daily. Essentially, be intentional

about developing strong and authentic relationships without thinking about the benefit to you.

2. **Rise above personal attacks/criticism:** In response to personal criticism and attacks, First Lady of the United States Michelle Obama once said, "When people go low, we go high." At all cost, do not respond to personal attacks, ridicule, or criticism from peers or any other stakeholders. The response from leaders who are demonstrating a high level of emotional intelligence will rise above the fray even when the attacks are intended to marginalize, and cause hurt. Yes, there are instances when people respond to pressures of not meeting a target or feeling threatened by your poise during the storm of apparent mission failure. This does not mean that you have to reciprocate. An empathetic and compassionate leader who embodies the philosophy of the Seven Second-Chance™ approach can face criticism and redirect the attacker or critic towards the team or organization's mission.

3. **Take Ownership:** Leaders who anchor their team's work in a theory of action that highlights shared responsibility and shared accountability will inevitably encourage mem-

bers of their team to take individual responsibility for failures and shortcomings. The leader who practices the Seven Second-Chance™ approach encourages reflection and taking personal responsibility without feeling the pressures of evaluation even though it exists. The morale of teams and organizations that encourage members to take ownership for failures and success alike, are likely to cultivate a culture of high morale and increased longevity amongst members. It is critical for leaders to demonstrate and model vulnerability and openly admit when they made a mistake. There is an increased likelihood for people to trust leaders who openly admit when they made a mistake.

4. **Believe that people have the best intentions:** In the education arena, there is a saying that "parents send us their best students" every day." Essentially, we operate from a place that does not assume that parents keep their best and brightest students and children at home and send us their most challenging ones to be educated. Similarly, in leadership, we should demonstrate a belief that people are committed and they are doing the best that they can now. Even when they are not meeting the exemplary mark based on the organization or team created rubric, the empathetic

and compassionate leader approach says that you must find a way to seek what might be the interference or impediment that a conversation and coaching can remove. Avoid thinking that a person is out to "get you," "incompetent," "lazy," "stupid," or "not as smart as you are" or they left their better selves at home or at the previous job. Take the time to find out why what you believe to be a simple task is not being executed well by them. Find out more about why they did what they did to help put them back on the right track. Leaders who embrace the Seven Second-Chance™ approach exercise empathetic leadership and balance it with shared accountability. Engage in a conversation that gets to the bottom of what the person feels about the task, what constitutes an excellent execution of efforts, or what they honestly believe to be their role in achieving an excellent outcome.

5. **Scalable leadership means supporting people's trajectory for growth and success:** The adage, "we want our children to exceed the achievements of their parents," is a solid yardstick for leadership. Self-actualized leaders and those who exercise empathy and compassion in their work create opportunities for their direct reports to exceed their accomplishments and surpass their status. These are leaders

who are what I call the "trajectory visionary." Like the way an excellent teacher has the ability to see a child's potential and what they can become and not judge and educate them based on who they are "now," leaders who embrace the Seven Second-Chance™ philosophy and empathetic leadership see the possibilities and potential in every employee who is under their tutelage. The major difference is that they recognize this potential, and are intentional about coaching, encouraging, and supporting these team members to achieve more and improve their own career and improvement aspirations. This is a sure way to scale leadership and overall organization improvement.

6. **Be quick to listen and slow to speak or act:** My mother would always remind us that there is a reason we have two ears and one mouth. She would say that this means you should listen more than you speak. Empathetic and compassionate leaders never aspire to be the dominant voice in the room or at the table. This leadership stance of listening more than you speak is even demonstrated during a time of crisis where they believe that solutions and answers are needed immediately. Rather than jump to premature conclusions, blame others, or shirk their responsibility regarding

the situation, they remain poised, composed, and anchor themselves in a solutions-oriented stance. As a principal supervisor in an era of "urgency for results," I almost never make any evaluative conclusions about a principal's leadership when they are not meeting their targets or goals before the first 60 to 90 days. Although this is counter-intuitive to the "sense of urgency" that plagues most contemporary organizations and teams, it is prudent to conduct a deep analysis and gather the appropriate information before speaking on their performance.

7. **Organizations/schools that desire fast solutions are almost ALWAYS in reform and reorganization mode.** We must operate with a "sense of urgency" is just another way of saying that we need a quick fix. I have rarely seen instances where the sense of urgency approaches, without well thought out strategic actions resulted in sustainable improvements and the achievement of the bottom-line. Surely, the empathetic and compassionate approach requires patience and a focus that is often unprecedented. The payoff is that it will build teams that learn to exhibit a high level of emotional intelligence. The "sense of urgency" is often impulsive and has a headstrong (intelligence quo-

tient approach), hard-nose approach that dangles evaluation and a performance matrix over the heads of employees. Conversely, the approach that taps into empathetic and compassionate leadership encourages the leader and team to be objective as they keep their emotions in check during difficult times. One such example is the inclination of school leaders and teachers to impart disciplinary consequences on students, or for school and district administrators to make evaluation decisions that negatively impact teachers. In these instances, I encourage teachers, staff, and school leaders to delay those often-immediate decisions and ask **seven questions** pertaining to the person who is at the end of the decision:

1. What is the home circumstance of the person?

2. What are the mitigating factors that resulted in the person's actions?

3. Has this behavior been displayed before and is it typical?

4. Is there a person in the building with whom the person has a positive relationship?

5. What are alternative decisions or consequences that I should consider?

6. What impact will my decision have on the person's life, the life of others who are connected to them, and the culture of the team or organization?

7. If I were at the other end of this decision, what would I want the consequence or decision to be?

The seven guidance points are not an exhaustive list of attributes that empathetic and compassionate leaders exhibit. There are seven points in which radically empathetic leaders can anchor their daily execution of responsibility. The leader who demonstrates an affinity for the Seven Second-Chance™ approach to their work is one who embraces and encourages empathy and compassion as a necessary tool to achieve the team or organization's bottom-line.

Jim's Story

"First year teachers take most of my time. I am constantly being called to their classroom and it seems like they never want to work through issues but rely on the school's administration for everything ..."

Jim was in his third year as the principal of a high performing middle school. We met because I was the keynote presenter at a conference he attended. Of course, my presentation was about the importance of leading with empathy and compassion. At the end of my presentation, he stood up and asserted that principals don't get paid to hold teachers' hands and care about how they feel. He shared that "principals exist to get students to achieve." I reached out to him for a follow up conversation and he agreed.

Due to a series of unforeseen events, we weren't able to connect for over a year. When we met Jim had changed his previous position and ideas as it pertains to what I had shared during my speech at the conference. This time he was quick to point out that "principals in some instances do exist to hold teachers' hands and guide them to improvement." Without nudging, he stated that he saw his school leadership role as one that included being a coach and guide, while attempting to strike a balance for accountability.

Jim shared that during the year that had passed since the conference, he had seen firsthand how he and his leadership team saw the benefit of investing in teachers who were not providing quality instruction to every student. He shared that in his readings, reflections from my teachings at the conference, and in conferring with peers who were leading other schools, the commitment to learn more about teachers than what is written on their resume was a game changer. He reached up to grab a large binder from a shelf in his office and handed it to me. The cover had the title "Skill/Will Chart of XYZ School Teachers. Jim explained that following the research of the categorization of employees based on their skill set, or willingness to be strong contributors to the work was the most effective approach for him. Teachers and staff who were categorized as being "High Skilled and High Willed were those who he considered exemplary. On the contrary, those teachers and staff who categorized as "Low skill/Low Will" were those who one year ago he was inclined to evaluate out or use the performance improvement plan out (PIP) as the instrument to do so. In the K-12 education arena, the term "PIPing out" is a practice whereby the school leader places the teacher or staff on a performance improvement plan for the sole purpose of showing why they are not a good fit and ultimately removing them from the school. Jim asked me to state what percentage of teachers I noticed in the Low Will/Low Skill category in his binder. I calculated and the number was 30%. He smiled and asked me if I believe that he can run a successful school with a 30% teacher turnover? I pointed out to him that his question must be rhetorical. He smiled and confirmed that it was. Jim assured me that he believes that the cavalry isn't coming, referring to the possibility of recruiting new teachers who he refers to as the calvary. We discussed the fact that his pivot towards investment, coaching, and development of the low performing teachers will yield dividends, and ultimately benefit students. I asked Jim if he remembers his first two years as a teacher. With a sarcastic tone, I asked him if he remembers how dynamic he was and knew everything about teaching. I then asked him if he would have hired himself when he was a first-year teacher. In response to the last question, he said that he probably would not have hired himself after his first-year performance. He leaned back in his chair, stared up at the ceiling for a minute, and then said, you are right. Some of our best teachers and now most effective leaders were not that great during their first year. I told him that many of them were not close to being good during their first few years and encouraged him to read "The Power of Seven Second Chances: Obtaining Success Without Firing the Rest." We both laughed, shook hands, and he said, "I got it!" I reminded Jim that a radical empathetic approach can be time consuming, challenging, and even burdensome when addressing the challenge of underperforming teammates, teachers, and staff but investing in people who have chosen this noble profession is always worth it.

The Necessary Shift
Toward Radical Empathy

Prioritizing people over practices is often a time consuming and burdensome pivot to make, but well worth it. Investing the time in learning who people are beyond their resume. School and district leaders should commit to learning more than what is on their teachers and staff resumes within the first 90 days of their employment at the school and district. The importance of investing in knowing about people beyond their resume is also applicable to any other professional pursuit. Establish a culture within your school or organization that permits failure and encourages opportunities for improvement and development. A failure tolerant culture is not a goal averse pursuit. On the contrary, a team or organization that has a culture which allows some failure and permits it is one that encourages teammates to take chances, discourages risk aversion, and innovates.

Chapter 12.

The "Blockbuster Effect" – Shifting the Paradigm of Leadership in Schools

School and district leaders are back at work, their much-deserved summer vacation is likely over, and the responsibility of educating, empowering, and enlightening more than 50 million students throughout the United States looms before them. In recent years, professional development or opportunities for capacity building for teachers, staff, and leaders at every level will be prioritized. The issue is the fact that in too many instances, the presentations, philosophy, and ideology being espoused are the same as the previous years. The content is often simply recycled. This is compounded by the fact that the low investment by many leaders is exacerbated by the unqualified presenters delivering the content. Based on the evidence that speaks to the state of K-12 education, the aforementioned conclusion holds true, and it is apparent we (educational leaders in America) are not achieving the **profit margin** that may restore the American school system to the preeminence in K-12 education it once held.

How can we mitigate this prevalence of mediocre practices (no shift in practices) that are being recycled each year with little impact on our education bottom-line? What lessons can school and district leaders learn from a movie and home entertainment company whose profit margin was negatively impacted because they refused to shift their practices? The issue with school and district leaders; this group of public servants who are engaging in the most important work of our time, is what I often refer to as the **"Blockbuster Effect"** in the ranks of leadership. Blockbuster was a multi-billion-dollar company ($5 Billion) in the 1980s, 1990s, and 2000s. Its franchises were the star retailer for home movie and video game rentals; and the most attractive after school and recreational endeavor for millions of children and adults.

Less than 30 years later, Blockbuster is non-existent, having closed its last store in January of 2014, and replaced by Fires-tick, Redbox, Hulu and Netflix; the company who attempted to innovate and shift Blockbuster's practices but was rejected. As in many instances in school and district leadership, there are opportunities to shift leader practice and to innovate in ways that are likely to increase the bottom line or profit margin; however, the "Blockbuster Effect" impedes the adoption of these attempts to shift.

In 2000, Reed Hastings, the founder of Netflix, approached Blockbuster with an offer to sell his company to them for $50 million. Blockbuster declined, as their leadership laughed at the

Netflix founder's proposal. Today, Netflix's is a **$28 billion** company. This explanation about Blockbuster's eventual demise is somewhat facile, does not delve into the complexities of their leadership shortcomings, and as it stands may not make my case for an alignment to school and district leadership. The truth is, an enormous part of Blockbuster's revenue was the result of the late fees that it charged its customers. During my own time as a customer, I subscribed to the late fee revenue stream. So, in the world that Netflix created, subscriptions and keeping a video/movie for as long as one wanted to, made the annoying Blockbuster late fees a thing of the past. What should school and district leaders learn from the Blockbuster-Netflix debacle? Although there are many leadership lessons within the model, I want to highlight one lesson from Netflix.

Netflix created a customer friendly model, and simultaneously **prioritized people over profits**. The prioritization of people over profits is another approach that is espoused in "The Power of Seven Second-ChancesTM." In the Netflix case, the customers were so pleased with the offerings; they started to refer friends, relatives, and even strangers to try it. Network scientists refer to this as the **Threshold model of collective behavior**. For any given and new idea, there are going to be people with varying levels of resistance. Once there is an established base of people who begin to adopt the new concept, the more resistant ones become more likely to join in. Once optimum conditions are created, a viral cascade can ensue. As we continue to think about what leadership and pedagogical moves are necessary to change the landscape of K-12 education, we have to stop recruiting, investing in, and believing in leaders who are suffering from the "Blockbuster Effect."

There are seven indicators that should resonate with leaders who are suffering from or have a diagnosis of the "Blockbuster Effect." It is important to note that a diagnosis is not a life sentence. If more than 50% of the indicators below resonate with you, you should be open to shifting your practice, and may do so by reaching out to my personal thought partners and consultants, Lively Paradox, at www.livelyparadox.com.

7 Indicators you are Suffering from the "Blockbuster Effect"

1. You are not a Culturally Responsive Leader. You disregard the beliefs, values, and traditions of your customer base in your strategic planning.

2. You do not have a social media account (IG, Snapchat, Facebook, Twitter)

3. You were politically elevated into a school or district leadership position, but you have never taught.

4. Your key strategies in which you anchor your daily practices are the same as they were 3 years ago.

5. You have a leadership team where 20% of the members influence 80% of the strategic decisions.

6. Your team/organization's mission, vision, and key strategies are not grounded in a customer friendly orientation.

7. Your actions perpetuate a systemic process of encouraging inequity, inequality, and discriminatory practices amongst your stakeholders.

Simply put, you are not deemed to be fair, empathetic, and consistent in your decision making. Before you dismiss these findings, consider how important it is to first acknowledge what is true and then start to think of how you can create change in each of the deficient areas. Remember, this is not a life sentence. By addressing these issues, you will have a chance to see the value of your staff in different ways that will lead you to an empathetic style of leadership.

Michelle's Story

Many people would describe Michelle as one of those individuals who changed how the business of education from a district leader's perspective should be conducted. She gained notoriety for firing principals on the spot, took no excuses for student achievement, and was accused of not having a heart, much less, an empathetic bone in her body. In spite of the fact that her reputation preceded her, Michelle's approach to change and not conduct the business of education the way it was conducted a decade prior to her role as the CEO of the district is a parallel to the Blockbuster-Netflix story. Michelle's approach to urban school district leadership was an approach unlike what occurred in many other places. She made it known that student success for all students was the district and school's most important priority. Her expectation was for the principal to take ownership for this priority, and any principal who did not demonstrate this would be out of a job.

Some may argue that her approach was devoid of empathy and compassion. I purport that she displayed some of the tenets of radical empathy from both the first and second 7 commitments (see leadership commitment #4). Her approach to shared accountability started with the leader on the ground and in charge of the school. She constantly stated that she expected parents and the mayor and city council to hold her accountable for the success of the district. As such, she was relentless around holding school leaders accountable, and she gained some of her notoriety after firing one such principal on national television.

It was the shortest interview ever! I was reluctant to say yes to the offer to move to Washington D.C. to serve as the principal of a school under Michelle's leadership. I was reluctant because I was serving as the principal of a school 45 minutes away in Baltimore City. A school where our students were resilient, smart, defying the odds, and doing so under the tutelage of an amazing group of teachers and leaders. I did not have a reason to say yes to this recruitment. Then it happened, I visited the school in Washington D.C., met several students, and they tugged at my heart strings. Two weeks later, I said yes to what I saw as an opportunity to replicate the work and successes that we had achieved in Baltimore at my current school. The final stage of the recruitment process was a one-on-one meeting with Michelle. She asked me why she should hire me to serve as the 10th principal in 8 years at this school? A school with a rich history of being a beacon in the community, and one where the alumni include many notables of our society. I responded that I could guarantee her that regardless of how long I serve in the role, the school and community will be better when I leave. With the same stoic look, she maintained throughout the interview, she asked if I had any questions for her. At this point, approximately four minutes into our interview, I took out my notepad expecting to write a couple of pages of expectations. I asked what was her expectation of me in the role as principal? Her reply, "keep us out of the news." The interview ended, and four years later, I had not met her one expectation. During my four years as the principal, the school made the news (television, print, and social media) dozens of times, 99% of which were positive and celebratory. Michelle never visited the school during my tenure, and that was the last conversation that she and I had. I wanted to make it clear to Michelle that I intended to bring a different form, approach, and type of leadership to the role. Like the Blockbuster-Netflix story, I did not want my leadership to reflect a paradigm from decades ago. I wanted her to know that vision to bring my leadership into the homes of those who we served, and to do so at minimal emotional, social, or financial cost to them.

While it is clear that one of Michelle's areas of growth included empathy and compassion, her clarity of expectations and commitment to student success for all were positives from her legacy. For many leaders who have the technical aspects of leadership as strengths, an orientation toward empathy is even more challenging. If I had the opportunity to sit across from Michelle today, I would ask what she could do differently to ignite her own inclinations for empathy and compassion.

Chapter 13.

A Race to the Finish Line

Sheila Madkins, the data guru, and passionate student advocate produced and shared information that immediately evoked a multitude of reactions from members of St. Louis Public School's Executive Leadership Team. The record-breaking violent crime rate she referenced in her presentation that day was public information and common knowledge. However, how she shared the information made it patently clear to anyone that there was likely a connection between the crime rate and the district's policies. The statistics surrounding the 203 murders that year generated many assumptions about the racial identity of the perpetrators and victims. The way Ms. Madkins unpacked this data and aligned it to the city's school system was powerful and enlightening.

In addition to her primary role in the district, Ms. Madkins served in a secondary role where she was an integral part of a sub-committee that I chaired while serving as the High School Network Superintendent of the district. The initial charge of this committee was to conduct frequent analysis of the school system's data in its 13 high schools and five alternative schools, identify existing gaps, and align appropriate strategies and tactics that would mitigate the areas of struggle, growth, and concern. We were named the Finish-Line For Life (FLFL) Committee. This name had its genesis in the belief that our primary goal was to get every student across the proverbial finish line of high school graduation, coupled with the fact that the work that we embarked upon was life changing and life altering for children and their families.

Because of this work, the St. Louis School District experienced many bright-spots and successes while the City of St. Louis recorded a record-breaking homicide year. Under the superintendent, Dr. Kelvin Adams who was in his tenth year in the role, the district was fiscally in the green, it regained full accreditation after 10 years, and several secondary schools were ranked in the state and nationally for their academic performance and preparation of students for post-secondary success.

The signal and message of the FLFL Committee to other stakeholders was clear; this school district's leaders and district leaders everywhere must be on the hook for the post-secondary failure of its students (graduates and non-graduates) as much as politicians and other city officials. Based on their analysis the FLFL Committee made several connections to the violent crime rate and the school system's practices that perpetuated systemic oppression and rampant racialized outcomes. One of those outcomes included a dismal drop-out rate. There were four metrics that spurred action:

- City's homicide rate

- High school drop-out rate

- Disproportionate student discipline data

- Attendance of high school seniors

In addition to myself and Ms. Madkins, the other members included several non-instructional leaders (Chief of School Security, Deputy Superintendent of Operations, Budget Director, District Auditor). We were intentional about bringing together a diverse group of people, perspectives, and experiences to tackle one of the biggest civil rights issues in the district and our larger community. An issue whose causes were firmly rooted in increasing the high school drop-out and push-out rates. The practice of expelling and suspending students inevitably fueled the school to prison pipeline. It was apparent that our children were pawns in the massive expansion of the prison industrial complex. What was clear to the FLFL Committee was that this was the result of pervasive systemic oppression, racialized outcomes, and the ultimate failure of marginalized students.

It did not take this FLFL Committee long to realize that these unconscionable occurrences in the district epitomized a microcosm of practices that were prevalent in the U.S. at large. During this time, there were members of the leadership team who magnified the challenges that marginalized students faced. They overtly and covertly made biased decisions that perpetuated microaggressions.

One inspiring fact was that I was leading many adults who were insistent on changing the system and calling out the others. Another inspiring finding and conclusion of the FLFL Committee was that many of the dismal student outcomes were not attributed to student capacity (student's academic deficits) or pedagogical delivery (teacher practice). On the contrary, there was overwhelming evidence that the prevalence of white privilege, an empathetic leadership drought, and a lack of culturally responsive pedagogy and leadership perpetuated these negative outcomes.

One example of privilege, bias, racism, and white supremacy came through the actions of a white executive team member. She engaged in a relentless push to discontinue the tennis team at Charles E. Sumner High School. If successful, her tenacity would have impacted the students negatively and eroded the rich history of one of the community's and America's greatest heroes and his legacy. What is ironic about the desire to dismantle the tennis team at Sumner is that the school's tennis court was named after one of its' most famous graduates, Arthur Ashe. Ashe was from St. Louis and the first African American to win Wimbledon and play on the United States Davis Cup Team. Recognizing the possible racialized aspect of this decision, I immediately opposed the decision. My grounds for blocking this decision were threefold:

1. I had spent an inordinate amount of time interacting with and supporting the principal, teachers, and students of the school, 99% of whom were African Americans.

2. I had seen and heard enough of the same actions and similar tactics by some of the district's central office and school leaders to systematically oppress most of the students of color, while elevating the successes of a selected few. These practices, some overt and others institutionalized.

3. My belief that disregards for the cultural and educational experiences of Black and LatinX students should not be allowed to be eroded without the acknowledgement, or

elevation of the voices and perspectives of those adults and students who represent the non-white St. Louis community.

The response to my objection was typical of the bold and brazen actions by some K-12 executives. My white colleague had the temerity to send an email in response to my rationale for opposing the discontinuation of the tennis team. In her email she reminded me that "I was not from around St. Louis and she was born and raised there." To her, the city of her birth was a legitimate reason for continuing pervasive racialized practices that are negative, and characteristic of schools and districts that serve Black and LatinX students throughout the United States. I did not respond in writing but knocked on her door and reminded her that wherever Black and LatinX people resided, that is where I am from.

The tennis team at Charles E. Sumner High School, the alma mater of Arthur Ashe and one of the best tennis facilities in the city of St. Louis, was discontinued on the grounds that the school could not field a coach. This is one of several examples of the perpetual systemic oppression that continuously marginalizes students in this and other urban districts. The FLFL Committee looked at this and many other examples of marginalization, said enough is enough, and took action to change the outcomes.

Action 1

The first action was to increase the awareness of the data that the FLFL Committee was privy to. We shared data from the National Center of Educational Statistics (NCES) and the Bureau of Justice Statistics affirming that our suspected correlation between the St. Louis's crime rate and student and school failure was correct. To strengthen the case, we specifically highlighted the work of the economist Lance Lochner who found that;

- 75% of violent crimes are committed by high school drop-outs

- More than 80% of inmates in state and federal prison did not graduate from high school, and

- For every 1% increase in the high school graduation rates of young men, the national crime data related to murder, aggravated assault, and auto-theft is reduced.

Also, a part of the awareness building, we shared our desired goals. The first was our desire to engage every high school student with a real opportunity to attend college. As expected, several members of the executive leadership team still did not want to accept the correlation between violent crime and the school district's dropout rate. As such, they did not demonstrate a propensity to treat it as a priority. The FLFL Committee did not criticize this reaction or lack of interest by the dissenting members of the executive team. We did attempt to understand their perspective and then moved forward with planning a tactical response to mitigate the issues that the high school students were faced with.

Action 2

The FLFL Committee created a strategic plan that was simplistic but grounded in SMART goals. Our intent was simple. The data pointed to perpetual systemic inequities and racialized outcomes throughout the district that many were aware of, but few were willing to address directly. This unwillingness to disrupt the status-quo, as with many K-12 institutions in America, should not be attributed to a paucity of resources. We believe that this is not a resource issue. It was, and continues to be simply a matter of true commitment to understand (empathy) why the disproportionate outcomes were so pervasive, and partner with key community residents, district, and school personnel to change it at all cost (radical empathy).

The FLFL Committee members were committed and decided to take action to mitigate the racial inequities that existed in this school system and city. In partnership with a local university, Harris Stowe State University, and its president and Director of Enrollment Management Dr. Dwaun Womack and Mr. Renaldo Brown, we embarked on a relentless campaign to create equitable college going and other post-secondary opportunities for students.

The following school year arrived and during the fall, the FLFL Committee and university president visited the high schools where they assembled and presented compelling cases for college attendance, and shared personal testimonies, and opportunities for college attendance with students. The attendees were particularly students who fell into the following categories:

1. Students who did not express an interest in college because they did not see the value in attending.

2. Students who were not encouraged to pursue college by their school officials because they had attendance or disciplinary issues.

3. Students who were first generation college students (potentially) and expressed an interest in alternative post-secondary pursuits.

At each of these 1.5-hour assemblies, several students were offered tangible incentives by President Womack and the St. Louis Public Schools FLFL Committee. The university officials in their generosity even offered full, four-year scholarships for some students. Word about this innovative and courageous program eventually made its way to other universities such as St. Louis' Washington University, whose officials expressed an interest in a partnership with the St. Louis Public Schools.

What is clear from the bold and demonstrative actions of this group of leaders was that creating the right conditions for planting the seeds of quality and equitable opportunities for marginalized students requires bold actions. It also requires an unapologetic naming of the issues amongst those in positions of power and influence, in and out of the systems that perpetuate them. The St. Louis Public Schools FLFL Committee saw measurable success with their initial cohort of over 100 students who would have otherwise fallen through the cracks by the time I left that district.

Lisa's Story

She wanted to make a difference. She had spent the past 25 years as a police officer where she moved up the ranks to that of captain, and decided after extensive career, she wanted to support the city's public school system; so, she said yes to serve as the head of their police department. In the 12 years of serving as the chief of police for the school district, Lisa had seen her share of students, particularly historically marginalized students pass through the annals of the criminal justice system, funneled into the school-to-prison pipeline, and even drop out of school. When the opportunity presented itself for Lisa to join a group of like-minded colleagues in the school district to address the systemic challenges that negatively impacted the aforementioned marginalized students, she said yes and made several adjustments to the way policing was done within the school district.

The radically empathetic practices that were implemented included police officers being required to visit the homes of 12th grade students who had significant absences or dropped out of school. The officers were encouraged to inquire from the students the reasons they were not coming to school and inform them of the options available to support them. These visits often resulted in some officers being assigned to provide transportation to the students if that was an issue or barrier that prevented them from attending school regularly. Lisa believed that her role and reputation and that of her department as the enforcers of the law needed to transcend the traditional school police student relationship. Her daily interactions with school personnel and students included her visits to schools and classrooms to speak with students, and on several occasions, she and her officers served as mentors and sponsors to several of the 12th graders in order to ensure that they remained in school and get them across the finish line. Lisa shared that she had seen too many instances where the system that was set up to protect and serve, perpetuated practices and kept structures in place that perpetuated punishment of the neediest students.

Two years after the formation of the Finish Line For Life (FLFL) Committee, Lisa retired from her position as the head of the school district's police department. Her retirement was disappointing to many adults and students alike. Her joining the team that collaborated around saving students who were at risk of not receiving a high school diploma or dropping out was Lisa's commitment to radically empathetic leadership. This shift towards radically empathetic leadership resulted in the significant improvement in the lives of those with whom she came into contact.

The Necessary Shift
Toward Radical Empathy

It became clear that Lisa prioritized a shift in her behavior that transcended the job description assigned to her role. Becoming a radically empathetic practitioner sometimes requires one to challenge the job description assigned to them. It requires an unselfish approach to existing whereby one prioritizes the happiness and joy of others over their own. Ask yourself if the work for which you awaken at 05:00 each morning is benefitting anyone other than you and your immediate family. If your answer is no, be intentional to change that way of existing in small and incremental ways. Finally, revisit and reexamine your social, professional, and even political affiliations. Are those who you admire or spend time with socially, professionally, or politically leading an unselfish existence? If the answer is yes, you have chosen your friends well. If the answer is no, you know what to do. You can do it.

Chapter 14.

What do Olympic Athletes and School Leaders have in Common?

In the 2016 season of the Olympic Games, I had a moment of reflection and nostalgia and decided to juxtapose the unlikely similarities between **Olympic athletes** and **school leaders** and for argument pose the question; how are school leaders/educators journeys parallel to that of Olympians?

1. **The lonely journey (a team sport with individual glory):** In preparation for the trials and eventually competition that pit the top 1% of the world's elite athletes against each other, Olympic athletes often find themselves in places of solitude that may transcend mental and physical spaces. Places that are emotionally tumultuous with very few trusted confidants and peers to whom they can turn. School and district leaders understand this all too well. The typical 14–16-hour work day that requires them to constantly give of their expertise and pour encouragement, inspiration, motivation, and love into adults, students, and families on a daily basis. As an Olympic athlete, a flinch, a moment of hesitation, the wrong leap, or a split-second decision can cost you your race/event and hopes of Olympic glory. Similarly, school leaders make an average of 500 decisions daily. During this time, if they do not make the most prudent and strategic decision during the daily execution of their roles

and responsibilities in America's schools, they can find themselves not missing the proverbial medal podium but affecting the lives of hundreds of students and adults with unfavorable outcomes.

2. **Repetition and practice:** Every Olympic athlete knows and appreciates that the multiple hours, days, weeks, months, and years of practice and repetition ultimately prepares them to respond in gold medal winning fashion when it really matters. Similarly, school leaders who are tremendously successful are those who appreciate and commit to the power of practice with instructional observations, feedback and coaching, practice positive engagement of the community and practice. They may also enjoy repetitions of executing and tweaking the implementation of their daily operational practices which includes practicing their speeches, and role plays for every situation as a school leader before it occurs.

3. **Public falls, fails, and sacrifice is a hallmark of Olympic athletes and school leaders alike.** These proverbial or metaphorical falls often result in scars of permanence that are visible, and sometimes invisible. What the well-prepared

Olympic athlete and school leader understands is that every fall is not a failure! Being well trained, and mission focused are the ingredients that allow gold medal Olympians and high performing School leaders to exercise resilient and situational leadership, which ultimately results in unprecedented achievement worthy of celebration.

4. **An unintended impact on lives:** Every four years, one unintended impact of the Olympic athletes' performance is that it inspires millions of people and gives young people and any aspirant an incredible sense of hope. Similarly, every decision that a school leader makes, can negatively impact the life of thousands of students, or inspire them to positive outlooks and improve their trajectory for achievement and success.

5. **Being a part of and leading Teams:** Although the United States has no doubt been the world's sprint power by having the most athletes ranked in the top 20 amongst the fastest sprinters in the world, the U.S. Olympic men's 4 X 100 track and field team has lost the last three major Olympic and World relay championships, primarily because the talent was not aligned to the team. Essentially, the team

has dropped or fumbled the baton in the most critical moments of exchange. As school leaders, it is understood that regardless of how talented or academically qualified one's team of leaders, teachers, and staff are, if the team is not mission focused and aligned, the result will inevitably be failure, and in some instances, incarceration and even death for our students.

6. **The four-year cycle:** I would respectfully submit that because we rally around our Olympic athletes every four years for a period of three weeks while they are on stage encouraging, cheering, applauding, forgiving, and even worshiping them; school and district leaders and teachers spend at least 180 days on stage every year, without the same level of support, applause, or accolades. As a former teacher, Olympic athlete, and school leader, I wonder how we would change the landscape of the United States K-12 education system if we treat and regard our educators similar to the way we treat and regard our Olympians. Would this result in our K-12 education system regaining the preeminence amongst the most developed countries that we once had in the 1970's and 1980's?

I can say without doubt, because I have experienced the amazing careers of being both an Olympian and an educator that they both deserve reverence, support, and radical empathetic leadership. Athletes are more than just bodies here to make the country proud and teachers are more than people who "fell back on" a career they never wanted. Both are champions!

Chapter 15.

The Joe Clark Story

TO BE CONTINUED...

Joe Clark, the real Joe Clark!

In the movie "Lean on Me," Academy Award actor Morgan Freeman, a brilliant thespian, displayed the real life of a hero of mine, a New Jersey school principal, Joe Clark. As an exemplar for radical empathy (empathy which often manifested itself through his unwavering commitment to his students regardless of their backgrounds and lived experiences) he was a hero until he died. When I started writing this conclusion, Mr. Joe Clark died at the age of 82 and he remains my hero.

Like millions of us around the world, I watched and was impressed, inspired by, and even angry at times at Joe Clark. The movie captured the real challenges and obstacles of the fictional and real character. Mr. Clark's school was at risk of being taken over by the New Jersey State government unless students improved their test scores on the state assessment. As with every radically empathetic practitioner, he did not allow politics to be prioritized over people.

I have had the unique opportunity to know him a bit more than reading about or witnessing his legend in the movie. I saw firsthand his continued display of radical empathy, compassion, love, and support. It certainly manifested itself through his support of his own children. I could see it particularly in the way that he engaged with his daughters who are amazing women and prolific Olympic track and field athletes. I had the honor of connecting and competing in the same spaces with them on many occasions. I share this because in the movie, there is no mention of Mr. Clark's family. However, he left an indelible mark on the lives of his children and offered a radical display of empathy that added value to the lives of students and teachers alike. According to his daughter, Hazel who is a friend and athletic peer of mine, "he never broke a promise, never let me down, and always believed in me."

Reading this book has likely left you with some of the emotions that I cautioned you about at the beginning, reflection, anger, inspiration, doubt, love. For many of us, making the necessary shift to become a radically empathetic leader may require a life altering occurrence. This journey to radical empathy could seem impossible, questions of whether it is worth the pursuit, inspired by trepidation of not knowing where to begin, or even wonderings about the why? My journey to become a radically empathetic leader was inspired by a life changing event. An event that changed my life and that of an amazingly talented student.

Capone's Story

Although I was oriented to empathy and compassion in my personal and professional pursuit, I believed that the moment that I became radically empathetic was in 2013. That year, I met one of my favorite students serving as a middle/high school principal. His name was Capone, named after the notorious gangster. Capone was a brilliant student-athlete. I remember his coach being stern and caring but holding him and his teammates to high expectations and watching him respond positively. Capone had a quiet disposition, but still had challenges fighting in and outside of school. Capone would often miss school for four days, show up on the fifth day, and then score better than 90% of his peers. He was talented in the classroom and on the court. Although I saw that potential, during my neophyte years as a principal, I did not always take the appropriate actions to activate and help him and other students to realize this potential.

During my first few years as a principal, my actions were manifested in a myopic focus of getting the students and school to achieve at unprecedented academic levels. In order to accomplish these academic goals, I displayed a zero-tolerance response to any students who impeded that goal and this included students who violated the school's code of conduct policy. I would suspend students for several days when they would have disciplinary infractions. In hindsight, I was not leading from a radical empathetic approach. In the movie *Lean on Me*, Joe Clark also made several decisions that are often misinterpreted as being radically empathetic. Those decisions were not radically empathetic, morally sound, or prudent. As we saw in the movie and understood from the real life of that dynamic school leader, suspending more than 300 students at any time in one's tenure is unacceptable and lacks any type of empathy. Additionally, radical empathetic leadership should not be devoid of a commitment to moral leadership. When one embarks upon the pursuit of school leadership, your life is forever altered. You are the public face of a revered institution. You can no longer go to the public places like the supermarket or place of worship without being recognized and held in high esteem. Given this, your decisions will reflect how you are perceived. Joe Clark's decision to bring strippers to the school was done with "good" intention, however, the impact was destructive, demeaning, and ill-advised. Radically empathetic leaders anchor their decisions in what is within the parameters of legal and moral.

As a first year principal, I would give out suspensions the way Oprah used to give away cars on her daytime television show. Whenever students violated the code of conduct, I would say, "You are all suspended." "You get two days." "You get five days." "You get seven days."

The challenge with this reflection, although accurate, is the fact that it negatively changed the lives of many students, especially one, Capone Chase. I received a call from my former assistant principal and friend. She asked if I had watched the news or read the Baltimore Sun newspaper. I told her that I had not seen the newspaper article or watched the news. From her voice, I could tell that something was seriously wrong. She was not only a school administrator, most of those students in the school referred to her as their second mother, and they respected her that way. Reciprocally, she treated, cared for, and loved them as her own children as well. One of the commonalities that she and I shared was our relentless commitment to our students. That morning, her phone call was to inform me that Capone's photograph was on the front page of the newspapers, and every television news station as "Public Enemy #1."

After being released from jail for an alleged burglary that they were involved with, Capone had approached one of his peers and co-defendant in Patterson Park only a few blocks away from the school, pointed a pistol at his head, confronted him about snitching (telling the police on him), directed him to get on his knees, and shot him in the face. He received the "Public Enemy #1" designation because he was on the run from law enforcement for capital murder. In less than one week, Capone was captured, tried, and subsequently sentenced to life in prison without the possibility of parole.

Despite his unbelievable academic and athletic ability and potential, Capone had dropped out of school. I often wondered about the impact on many of my students of my zero-tolerance practices based on the school district's zero-tolerance policies. Capone was no exception. It came to head at that moment and for years to come, that I had contributed to Capone's destiny. I had the ability and platform to be a Contributor or Combatant of the school to prison pipeline, and in those moments, unfortunately I chose to be a contributor. My radical empathy muscles had not yet been developed, and it cost one child his life. But it also cost one of the most brilliant students I ever met his freedom changing his life and mine forever.

In his first year of incarceration, I sent financial support and placed money on his books. Additionally, I have made several attempts to visit him at the North Branch Correctional Institution "hyper-max prison" in Allegany County, Maryland. I am committed to continue to reach out to secure a visit. A critical step in evolving towards a radically empathetic person is to take ownership when your decisions have negatively impacted the lives of others, and if possible, taking steps to make amends.

Chapter 16.

The Roadblocks to Radical Empathy

Our lived experiences have taught us that whenever we choose to make personal life altering decisions, the inevitability of barriers, impediments, or roadblocks will appear. Sometimes they appear in ways that we feel as if we are not built to handle them. Whether you are inspired by the life of a world-renowned figure such as Mahatma Gandhi, Martin Luther King, Jr. or someone in your circle whose life has displayed empathy, there is one thing that is clear. Regardless of where someone lands on the continuum of empathy, the level of enthusiasm required to pivot towards a radically empathetic orientation will require much reflection and deliberate action. The following road-blocks are inevitable, but many people have moved them out of the way towards empathy success. You can, too.

Politics and Political Pressure

We have seen and heard many discussions about the necessity for empathy and compassion in our society. Daniel Goldman reminds us that in the field of study of social-neuroscience and examination of empathy, there are three kinds of empathy. The first is *cognitive empathy* and this is where the adage of walking a mile in someone else's shoes comes to light. Exhibiting this type of empathy manifests itself in ways that shows your commitment to understand someone's mental models. You are willing to speak their language and embrace aspects of their culture. If one is devoid of cognitive empathy, this often leads to poor communication and the inability to make positive connections with others. He posits that it's impossible to succeed in the world without cognitive empathy.

The second type of empathy utilizes what neuroscientists call *the social brain*. This is where you are attentive and willing to establish rapport with others. Exhibiting this type of empathy requires one to make authentic emotional connections. The third type of empathy is sometimes referred to as *empathic concern*. This is where the action of being radically empathetic comes to light. Empathic concern is synonymous with radical empathy in that it requires one to have a willingness to help others once they realize that help is needed. In exhibiting this type of empathy, if you find out that someone's situation requires support, you will commit the time to mitigate it.

Ego

Being egotistical has not served humans well. By its simplest definition, ego is a person's sense of self-esteem or self-importance. Alex Watson describes the ego as marginal and impotent and aligns with autonomous thinking because it lacks power and knowledge. The textbook definition based on the Freud psychoanalytic theory of the Id, Ego, and Superego, the ego is that part of the mind that mediates between the conscious and the unconscious and is responsible for reality testing, and a sense of personal identity. Egotistical humans usually show up in ways that give one the impression that they are existing in an alternate reality. The ego often inspires some people to resist or discard feedback and encourages you to exaggerate your own ability. Essentially, if you walk around believing that you are better than everyone else, it is likely that you will not be able to be radically empathetic towards others.

Lack of Confidence

There are many instances when a person may not have the level of confidence in their abilities while serving or playing in certain arenas. Starting a new job in a similar role in which you have served for two, twelve, or even twenty years with much success can still have you questioning your abilities to be your best self and excel in your given role. Having to navigate these new spaces can result in you not having a willingness to dish out doses of empathy to those with whom you come into contact. It is one's ability to give away as much empathy, knowledge, and support as you can and still maintain it all. Lacking confidence in your abilities can on occasion inspire you to hoard your emotions and capacity to help others. Conversely, those who are confident often take the position of, "I can give this away and still have it. I will help you even though I don't quite understand why you are struggling with this issue. We can do this together."

Traumatic or Other Past Experiences

Having personal or professional experiences where you were not the beneficiary of empathy when you should or could have can leave a bitter taste and erode your willingness to be an empathetic person. We are reminded that "hurt people, hurt people." A classic case where this tends to manifest itself is in scenarios where people who were deprived of empathy, deprive others of empathy. In many instances, individuals who are placed in positions and situations whereby they can add value to the lives of others if they orient themselves to understanding the needs of those individuals. Too often you may hear them say, "Well, when I was a first-year student, or when I joined this team, no one helped me." That is one of the clearest signs of someone whose trauma or experience created an empathy grinch. Having had traumatic experiences can result in you carrying the baggage of a lack of empathy. This can make you exhibit emotions such as anger and self-pity. Most of us have encountered someone with this disposition, and when we do, we should commit to showering them with empathy.

Selfishness

Self-serving pursuits will inevitably inspire those to exclude the feelings or lived experiences of friends, colleagues, and certainly strangers. Displaying a selfish disposition can result in one overlooking the struggles and issues of others because they believe that trying to help those individuals may result in added burden of their issues, thereby having a contagious effect and become their burden. Being selfless in your personal or professional pursuit allows you to build the radical empathetic muscles and give it out naturally. One example is the reluctance to share the steps that they took to achieve success or accomplish in an unprecedented way. The belief that doing so will reduce your own success or enable others to surpass you is potentially destructive.

Taking it Personal

In his bestselling book, "*The Four Agreements: A practical guide to personal freedom,*" Don Miguel Ruiz reminded us in one of the agreements; "Don't take anything personally" that nothing that people say or do to us is personal, but we must possess the self-confidence and know who we are to be ok with it. Developing the ability that allows you not to take anything person requires you to acknowledge that absolutely nothing people do or say about you is really about you. It is often about their own lived experience and stuff. On my own journey of becoming a radically empathetic leader, I have learned to become self-aware by reflecting on my own journey, understanding my own truth, and reassuring myself that it is not the name that I may be called by, or what I am told of myself by others, but what I respond to and how. The second agreement that Don Miguel Ruiz suggests that most people's actions towards you is because of something that they are dealing with in their own lives, and it's their way of projecting it on you. If you choose or learn how to ignore it, you will be in such a good space. Ruiz describes it as residing in "heaven on earth" while the other person resides in "hell on earth."

As you enjoy this journey of becoming or improving your radical empathetic orientation, I encourage you not to wait for a life altering experience. While there are no vaccines or medical technology to immunize against a lack of empathy, there are many children and adults who are waiting to benefit from your displays of radical empathy in the name of diversity, equity, and inclusive practices. Just make it happen!

Radical Empathy Survey

The survey questions are designed to gauge your empathetic and compassionate leadership orientation. Rating Scale:

4   Mastery/Effectively Empathetic

3   Proficient/Empathetic

2   Progressing/Somewhat Empathetic

1   Need/Lacking Empathy

Personal Leadership

I evaluate my own practices to gauge efficiency and effectiveness in teaching and/or leadership.

| 4 | 3 | 2 | 1 |

I believe I can grow.

| 4 | 3 | 2 | 1 |

I set or influence the tone for all stakeholders and adult relationships and practices in the organization.

| 4 | 3 | 2 | 1 |

My style strikes a balance between being very firm about non-negotiables and being flexible about how the work gets accomplished to leverage peoples' strengths.

| 4 | 3 | 2 | 1 |

I am clear about my expectations so that all stakeholders can do their best work.

| 4 | 3 | 2 | 1 |

I delegate as a means to develop my people and foster collaboration.

4   3   2   1

I relentlessly provide support and follow up to ensure targets are being met.

4   3   2   1

I demonstrate genuine engagement with others, humility, and relationship-building.

4   3   2   1

I own the team's failure and growth.

4   3   2   1

I am committed to recognize that people truly matter; my daily actions and leadership stances are a clear indicator that I believe this.

4   3   2   1

Resilient Leadership

I am willing to exhaust efforts at building capacity.

    4   3   2   1

I work to correct performance deficits in peers and colleagues.

    4   3   2   1

I am aware of the impact my teaching and leadership style has on my people.

    4   3   2   1

I consistently work to learn and understand the needs of my people.

    4   3   2   1

I make multiple attempts to use the strengths of my people to achieve operational excellence.

    4   3   2   1

I prioritize development.

4   3   2   1

I create, implement, and institutionalize sustainable systems
and processes that support professional development.

4   3   2   1

Culturally Competent Leadership

I examine my own biases.

4   3   2   1

I revisit my own dispositions, and biases with the goal of becoming more efficient and effective for daily operational excellence.

4   3   2   1

I continuously dismantle inequitable and exclusionary practices as I teach and/or lead.

4   3   2   1

I create a fully inclusive environment where all stakeholders, regardless of ethnicity, race, ability level, or other social constructs thrive and learn at high levels.

4   3   2   1

I am aware of my own cultural worldview and attitude towards cultural differences.

4   3   2   1

I am knowledgeable of different cultural practices and worldviews, and cross-cultural skills.

4   3   2   1

I possess a high level of cultural competency and teach/lead effectively across cultures.

4   3   2   1

I create equitable practices recognizing that inequity is pervasive in the arena of education.

4   3   2   1

I am committed through daily actions to diligently provide opportunities for equity and quality in the workplace.

4   3   2   1

Interpersonal Leadership

I build trusting relationships with everyone regardless of race, ethnicity, or other orientation.

4	3	2	1

I celebrate/credit my subordinates for team/organization success and goal achievement.

4	3	2	1

I am committed to publicly praise.

4	3	2	1

I am committed to privately correct colleagues for ineffective practice/underperformance.

4	3	2	1

I facilitate active stakeholder communities dedicated to achieving the organization's mission.

4	3	2	1

I have a relentless belief that everyone can continuously grow.

4   3   2   1

I can see beyond deficits and recognize possible contributions regardless of an individual's academic, behavioral, or social deficits.

4   3   2   1

I am successful at developing, building, and supporting healthy teams.

4   3   2   1

I believe that everyone should be invested to execute the mission and vision of the organization.

4   3   2   1

I practice shared accountability by not letting under performers off the hook.

4   3   2   1

I am intentionally discouraging high performers/achievers from becoming professionally aloof.

4   3   2   1

I am committed to the empowerment, encouragement, and uplifting of colleagues in an effortless manner.

4   3   2   1

I am committed to correct, or if necessary, chastise, violators of company policy (non-negotiables) in a manner that will not strip away dignity.

4   3   2   1

Score Chart

140+

You likely have a strong balance of empathetic & compassion ate leadership. This is a great place to be as a leader. We need more people with radically empathetic orientations who can help coach and develop more people to embrace empathy as a competitive advantage. Be certain that you help to bring others along.

105 – 139

You have an inclination to lead with empathy and compassion. You have many areas where you allow empathy to guide your decisions. It appears that you might also have trouble balancing radical empathy with logic and reason at times. Keep working at being consistent.

70 – 104

You have clear empathetic and compassionate developmental areas. These developmental needs may be attributed to your lived experiences, unearned privileges, or unwillingness to accept where you landed on the continuum. A shift will require some intentionality on your part or that of a coach.

69 or below

It appears that you are a leader with compassion deficits. It's ok. Many people have empathy issues and they are never made aware of them. When making decisions, consider seeking advice from a person who has greater levels of empathy than you. This will help to ensure that people don't suffer while you work to get it right.

Notes

Works Cited

Bloom, P. (2016). *The perils of empathy*. The Wall Street Journal.

Brown, B. (2018). *Dare to lead*. New York. Random House.

Goldman, D. (1998). *Working with emotional intelligence*. Bantam Books.

Hammond, Z.L. (2015). *Culturally responsive teaching and the brain*. Corwin Press.

Kendi, I.X. (2017). *Stamped from the beginning: The definitive history of racist ideas in America*. Nation Books.

King, R. (2018). *Mindful of race: Transforming racism from the inside out*. Sounds True Inc.

Moore, W. (2011). *The Other Wes Moore: One name, two fates*. Spiegel & Grau.

Noguera, P. (2008). *The trouble with black boys: And other reflections – race, equity, and the future of public education*. Jossey-Bass.

Price, N.D. (2019). *Cultivating culture as a garden*. Kindle Direct Publishing.

Price, N., Roberts, I. (2015). *The power of seven second chances: Obtaining success without firing the rest*. Kindle Direct Publishing.

Roberts, I.A. (2015). *Prisoners or presidents: The simple things that change everything when principals lead like lives depends on it.* Xlibris.

Ruiz, D.M. (1997). *The four agreements: A practical guide to personal freedom.* Amber Allen Publishing Company.

Sinek, S. (2011). *Start with why: How great leaders inspire everyone to take action.* Penguin.

Steele, C.M. (2010). *Whistling vivaldi: how stereotypes affect us and what we can do.* W.W. Norton.

Stevenson, B (2015). *Just mercy: a story of redemption.* Penguin - Random House.

Wallace Foundation & Washington University, (2015). *Model Principal Supervisor Professional Standards.* Council of Chief State School Officers.

Watson, A. (2014). *Who am I? The self/subject according to psychoanalytic theory.* https://doi.org/10.1177/2158244014545971

Wallace Foundation & Washington University, (2015). Model Principal Supervisor Professional Standards.

Watson, A. (2014). Who am I? The self/subject according to psychoanalytic theory.

About the Author

Dr. Ian A. Roberts, at the time of publishing, serves as the superintendent of Millcreek Township School District in Pennsylvania and is the Chief Thought Partner of Lively Paradox, a leadership development company based in the Midwest. In past years he has also served as the Chief Schools Officer for Aspire Public Schools, where he led the team of superintendents and associate superintendents whose focus was continuous improvement across K-12 schools in four regions (Bay Area, Central Valley, Los Angeles, and Memphis). Prior to this role, he served as the High School's Network Superintendent with Saint Louis Public Schools, where he coached, supported, and evaluated high school and alternative schools' principals, providing them with intensive coaching for effectiveness, excellence in student and teacher achievement outcomes, and cultural responsiveness; rather than for compliance. He encourages district leaders and principals with whom he works to think creatively about how they can improve their school communities, coupling research and his practitioner's experience in innovative school improvement and turnaround ultimately providing all with quality, equitable educational opportunities.

He served as a school turnaround principal and principal-manager where he and his team of teachers, staff, and community members, successfully turned around; as measured by student academic and behavioral achievement, college acceptances, teacher retention, and reduction in issues of disproportionality impacting students of color in what were once failing and persistently dangerous schools in Baltimore City, Washington, D.C., the South Bronx, New York, and St. Louis, Missouri.

He has successfully matriculated in and completed educational programs at Coppin State University (Undergraduate studies), St. John's University and Georgetown University (graduate studies), Morgan State University (Doctoral studies), and Harvard University (post-doctoral educational and leadership studies). Dr. Ian Roberts is a pivotal intellectual voice in the K-12 arena and is sought after throughout the United States and internationally to speak and lead sessions for organizational leaders on the power of empathy, compassion, and cultural responsiveness for organizational success. He blends credible research of pedagogical theorists with the educational practitioner's perspective. He is the author of three books on leadership, each of them having a focus on issues of equity, empathy, and culturally responsiveness. Prior to becoming a principal, district leader, and leadership consultant, Dr. Roberts was a world class and Olympic athlete. He competed in track and field at the 2000 Olympic Games in Sydney, Australia, Pan American Finals in Winnipeg, Canada, and World Championships in Maebashi, Japan and Seville, Spain.

LEARN MORE ABOUT THE AUTHOR AT:

@anadoctor2010_ian_roberts

@livelyparadox

www.livelyparadox.com

Made in the USA
Monee, IL
15 December 2024

74143736R00129